Table of contents

Introduction

Introduction: Hyena! and the work of queer mourning

Hyenas get a pretty bad press: in Egypt, during the reign of Ramesses XI, the year 1090 became known as the Year of the Hyenas. It was a year defined by climate disaster – drought, crop failure – starvation, and civil unrest. The appellation is both literal and political. Hyena populations felt the knock-on effects of the drought, and sought to scavenge food within the precincts of human habitation. In this way the hyena became viscerally identified with famine and disease in the ancient Egyptian imagination. 'Hyena' also conflates these animal harbingers with the feral behaviour of human beings, with a starving populace on the brink of revolution, devolving into chaos.

Hyenas are, according to most classical sources: loathsome and savage, insatiable of appetite, offensive of smell; they are cowardly but vicious, morally and spiritually unclean.

Pliny the Elder tells us that hyenas are the only animal to dig up graves in order to eat the corpses. In legend and folklore from around the world the hyena is a haunter of cemeteries; a devourer of the dead, the mount of witches.

But the hyenas of legend have other strange properties too: they have eyes of many colours, and dogs are struck dumb when the shadow of a hyena falls on them; any animal that looks at a hyena three times will be unable to move, says Pliny. And Ovid offers us this: 'We might marvel at how the hyena changes function, and a moment ago a female, taken from behind by a male, is now a male'. St Isidore of Seville writes of a stone to be found in the hyena's eye; if taken and placed under the tongue this stone will induce a man to prophesy the future.

There is something magical and not necessarily benign about the hyena. It shifts between categories of species and of sex. Neither male or female, neither cat or dog. It is said to prey upon the weak, but it is also a cipher for them: the hyenas of folklore have a symbolic affinity with the disorderly and dying, the sick in mind and body, the malcontented and the maimed. This negative iconography is deeply rooted and enduring. In 1923 a striped hyena from the San Diego Zoo was hired by Dorothy Davenport for the lost propaganda film *Human Wreckage*. The hyena was to represent the 'wasted spirit' of one ravaged by addiction, a metaphor invoked in the title of several contemporary tales of narcotics, crime, and opportunistic savagery. The hyena, like the addict, is weak but cunning, an indiscriminate scavenger. The hyena like the addict is 'immoral' and 'dirty', not merely wicked but squalid; repulsive yet pitiable. The addict is no longer a person, they undergo a radical transformation.

Therianthropy – the magical metamorphosis of human beings into animals – is one of the oldest folk beliefs. In the Cave of the Trois-Frères in south-western France there is a pictogram dating back to around 13,000 BC that appears to show a shaman figure in the process of animal transformation. The notion of hyena therianthropy is common in parts of North Africa and the Horn of Africa, and these legends are unusual because unlike other therianthropes, who started life as human beings, hyenas can disguise themselves as people. In the Middle East striped hyenas have traditionally been regarded as the physical incarnations of malevolent Jinns. And the13th Century Persian writer Zakariya al-Qazwini in his book *Marvels of Things Created and Miraculous Aspects of Things*

Existing describes a tribe of 'Hyena People', stating that if one of this tribe should be hidden in a crowd of 100, a hyena alone could sniff them out and devour them. They walk amongst us. They eat their own.

A great collector of therianthropic lore was Charles Hoy Fort, the well-known researcher into 'anomalous phenomena'. In his final book, *Wild Talents* (1932), Fort writes about the belief that under certain emotional conditions, such as grief or rage, a man might turn into a hyena. Literally. My friend, editor and mentor Roddy Lumsden had a lifelong interest in all things Fortean. It was something that united us. By strange coincidence, I was rereading bits of *Wild Talents* in the week before he died, and thinking about the hyena as an avatar for certain kinds of desire or emotional experience. The news of Roddy's death was a shock to my system – one shock in a long series of shocks – and it triggered something in me where, following a period of loss and turbulence, I'd reached a state in which animal transformation felt plausible to me, where I felt just mad enough and feral enough to turn into a hyena myself.

Mourning, I suppose, is a process or set of processes whereby all the raw, regressive anarchy of grief is absorbed back into articulate narrative language. It's a process of mediation and assimilation through which the individual is able to communicate their experience of grief, first to their family and friends, then to their wider community, and on, to society at large. We have many rituals aimed at producing rational, linear trajectories of grief – the obituary, the wake, the funeral, the eulogy, the elegy – and all these discourses – therapeutic, clinical, and literary – that attempt to move you towards a kind of recuperation; that want to socially situate your grief. All of which is helpful and necessary, but I also think there are kinds of grief, and that there are certainly grieved for subjects, not accommodated by those trajectories or rituals of mourning.

There are those society doesn't account as grievable, and there are some kinds of grief society doesn't want. How to mourn *those* subjects? And what to do with an experience of loss that is so disturbing and persistent that it can't be adequately reclaimed by language?

I began to search for a word or phrase to describe what I'm trying to do with my poetry, for the feelings and experiences I'm attempting to make space for. When talking about Hyena! I started to speak tentatively about a work of 'queer mourning', about poetry as a making space for the troubling strangeness that grief initiates in us. I tend to think of grief as a queering of the real, as a making strange of the world and the self to the self and the world. The character of Hyena! emerged because the accumulative effects of grief were a kind of therianthropy for me.

The hyenas of legend and lore were strange, fluctuant, threatening beings. There were moments, experiencing grief, when my own body felt strange and dangerous to me. I was changing my body in ways both involuntary and conscious: I couldn't eat, I couldn't sleep, I shaved my head. The magnitude of my feelings both provoked and demanded these changes, a remaking and remapping at the physical level. I am not the first woman to feel this way. To find, at times of great loss or stress, all her 'normal' bodily functions suspended, caught in arrest or revolt. The body behaving in this way is threatening to others too, wayward and ungovernable: the body that cannot bear to be touched, the body that must be touched, full of intense and compulsive desires, the body that shrinks or expands into 'ugliness', the body whose period stops, the body whose gums bleed; the body that resists any attempt at erotic instrumentalisation. The body that will not be managed. At our most abject we are often at our most revolutionary.

In 1957 the artist and occult practitioner Marjorie Cameron painted *The Vampyre*, also known as *The Beast*. It features a central female figure on all fours against a black background, experiencing some form of therianthropic transformation. The figure, anorexic and deformed, twists between the human and the animal, the fragile and the grotesque. It excites both sympathy and repulsion. It has a hyena-like mane of red hair. Cameron, as she preferred to be known, made this picture during a long period of mourning for her husband Jack Parsons. It is as eloquent as any art I've ever seen in describing that sense of alienation, awkwardness and loathing with and inside of yourself, a queering of your own shape and substance.

The queer, I think, is an identity or mode of being that is imperfectly held within language; it is an identity that cuts across and partakes of multiple categories of vexed belonging. The hyena is a cat and a dog, an animal, man, and a spirit; the hyena is male, then female at will. This is something I connect to my sexuality, of course, but also to culture and to class identity, to the feeling that has persisted all of my life of being, simultaneously 'both' and 'neither; to finding no perfect expression of solidarity, no true 'home' in any one territory or lexical field. Grief does this also, it destabilises you, it upsets and scatters your points of reference. To talk about death, or to talk about sexuality, we frequently resort to endlessly abstract and multiplying euphemisms; to cipher and slang and code. Language itself becomes strange as the known world tilts on its y axis.

Grief changes how we see and say, everything gets magnified, sensitised, brought into weirder, sharper focus. It changes what it is possible to think and to know; the words in which and through which we apprehend reality. In this state communication becomes complicated, the way we interact and understand one another changes. This relational uncannying is something I've always thought of as being part and parcel of the queer: the need to find new names, a new language in which we can speak our strange truths back to one another.

Hyenas have a language, or they have a kind of complex anti-language comprised of 'giggles', whoops, howls, and groans. These sounds have a kinship to those produced at the disruptive hiccuping core of human trauma; to the collapse of articulate speech that occurs when our rhetorical resources are utterly exhausted. It is not so much that trauma silences its sufferers, but that it begins in them a compulsive and repetitive need to speak: to gab and garble, jibber and slur, to laugh and cry, to be discursive and sullen in turns, and yet to come to the end of their invention without ever reaching or naming the *thing* they are trying to describe. It is not the case that trauma is or must remain 'unspoken', rather that any attempt at intelligent representation fails at, or is failed *by*, the limits of language. This is the difference between *articulate* and *eloquent.* When words won't do, we recruit gesture, the body, guttural non-verbal noises.

The hyena's laugh is repeatedly miscast and mischaracterised in folklore and contemporary culture alike as demonic, hysterical, or mocking. So too are the sounds of grief and trauma misunderstood. Women's grief especially. I began to see – or at least to imagine – a thread of connection between the hyena's laugh and the practice of the caoin, which exists in popular consciousness as a species of pagan noise-making. This misrepresentation was fostered by religious and occupying authorities in Ireland, who frequently demonised its practitioners as animalistic, immoral, or crazed, when in reality the caoin belongs to a highly complex and specific verse tradition, one with its own rich set of tropes, its own particular aesthetic disposition. Historically, criticisms of the caoin performed a kind of Janus-faced manoeuvre in which it was simultaneously despised for being heathen and wild, and disdained as 'immoral', because it ritualised – and sometimes monetised – the process of grieving. The caoin was too unrestrained and artless to be quite proper, while at the same time too formalised to be authentic or sincere. For the women who practised the caoin there was no way to win, and because the caoin was embodied to such a high degree, condemnation of the form also attached to those who performed it. It wasn't simply that the tradition of the caoin was in some way disorderly or 'bad', but that these qualities were also the signal moral attributes of the women who participated in it.

Hyenas are misunderstood animals. I don't suppose there is a woman alive who wouldn't feel some sense of kinship with their abjection and vilification, but it must be felt most deeply by the women who are 'other' even in the otherness of being a woman, women who are told they are mad, or perverse, or profane, for the ways they desire and the ways the grieve, women who are made to feel like animals. Witch belief is alive and well in many parts of the world, where rumours of animal transformation still attend accusations of witchcraft. The witch has her familiars: the bat, the owl, the toad and the hyena. And the witch takes on some of their properties, she sheds her own skin and becomes a beast.

Not a 'useful' beast either, a thing that cannot be harnessed, a thing that cannot be used for food or fuel, a thing that refuses rational control, that belongs to and in its own frightening magical world.

Therapists talk a lot about the 'magical thinking' initiated by an experience of profound loss; how everything becomes signs and portents, auguries and omens. In a sense this was always my world. I have never *not* been aware of being strange, of perceiving and interpreting my experiences in ways at variance to those around me. Does that make me mad? Magic, Silvia Frederici tells us, was a huge stumbling block to the rationalisation of the work process. It functioned as a kind of refusal of work, it was a form of insubordination and grass-roots resistance. The world – and women – had to be forcibly disenchanted before it – and they – could be dominated. Women's claim to magical power undermined state authority; it gave the poor and powerless hope that they could manipulate and control the natural environment, and by extension subvert the social order. So magic must be demonised, must be persecuted out of existence. If Hyena! is a witch then the poem is a spell. It is that scene of hope whose ambition is to overcome the horrible logic of death and the impossible demand to 'heal' from loss, to be made 'useful' again.

A poem is a space for magic, is a space in which my lateral leaps of logic can be encountered on their own terms; in which they have value and meaning, and in which they may find some measure of acceptance and fulfilment. By which I mean poetry proposes a territory, a zone of suspension from the habitual sense-making etiquette of daily discourse. Hyena! doesn't have to 'make sense' exactly, or 'live in the real world', she makes her own meaning, defiantly and loudly.

It's one of life's many little jests that what poetry as art accommodates, poetry as social scene does not. Although the writing of poetry holds profound sweetness for me, I've often felt the work I want and need to make is sidelined within certain strands of contemporary lyric practice. Hyena! has no patience for that, for being cleaned up or 'understood' or playing nice. Hyena! is often a burlesque of extrovert misanthropy. But this is grieving too, that bottomless, directionless rage that sucks in and consumes everything else. This kind of rage is not much wanted in lyric practice or 'civilised' company. It isn't very feminine, and it isn't very marketable.

Hyena! possesses a number of qualities I wish I possessed:

she says exactly what she thinks for a start; she doesn't prioritise other people's warm fuzzies over her need to speak her pain. She isn't embarrassed by her desires or disgusted by her body. Sometimes theriathropy might come as a relief.

One of my favourite short stories by Leonora Carrington sees a hyena attending a stifling debutante ball in place of her human friend. The hyena rips off the face of a maid in order to create a credible human disguise. While at the ball she behaves exactly as she pleases and has a marvellous time, but ends by revealing her true identity and leaping through a window, causing embarassment and shame to the girl's human parents. I think Carrington felt a strong identification with hyenas too. A smiling striped hyena appears in her *Self-Portrait* painted in1937. Both Carrington and the hyena stare out of the canvas with a direct, almost confrontational gaze. The figure of Carrington, seated, lifts a tentative left hand toward the hyena. The hyena lifts her left forepaw towards Carrington in a gesture of acknowledgement and recognition. 'I'm like a hyena' Carrington told an interviewer in 1999, 'I get into the garbage cans, I have an insatiable curiosity.'

Many of the women artists I admire have felt an affinity for hyenas, for all animals really, picturing themselves as and with horses, dogs, birds, monkeys, deer and tigers. What male scholarship and imagination condemns or denounces, female creativity draws strength from, donning their animal attributes like a cloak of power.

The very qualities in hyenas that have been the subject of anxiety and scorn are also – I think – their greatest strengths. This is often the case for women too, for working-class women in particular, and this is evident in the treatment of our art. Acknowledging a hyena's 'low cunning' and 'scavenging' nature is to admit, without ever having to credit, their intelligence, resourcefulness, and resilience. By figuring their laughter as idiot or lunatic a complex language is rendered as a witch's cackle. To see the hyena as a harbinger of starvation and sickness is anthropocentrically bigoted, when it is human encroachment and destruction of the hyena's natural environment that has driven them into such fraught contact with people. Similarly, the vocabulary that attends critical discussion of art and literature by women frequently descends into an orgy of faint-praise and routine dismissal. Particularly when the woman in question is neither beautiful, posh, or young.

Who is having these thoughts? Fran, or Hyena!? Once out of the box she would not go back in. And maybe she shouldn't. Maybe the Molotov of grit and gold she is able to draw forth is what is needed now, in my own poetry, and in poetry in general. Maybe it is only in borrowing some of her rage and strangeness that I can begin to craft a response to a world in and with which it feels impossible to reconcile.

Hyena! says nothing is solved. Not my anger and sadness at Roddy's passing, nor my anger and sadness at the other griefs that come crowding in its wake, gnawing at memory. Hyena! and I are not alright. Not even close. We're not, in point of fact, all anything. Ours are the borderlands, the edges, the liminal places. But we're not exiles. We are – we have become – comfortable here, and we've started to build something here with others like ourselves. We have been in that other world, the 'real' world, and although we know we can survive it now, it isn't our home. Our home is the elsewhere. We're visitors here. That sound you can hear? What you would call laughter? That is our language, our true poetry, Hyena! and I reporting back.

Hyena! Jackal! Dog!

Hyena!

Hyena! Jackal! Dog!

Tzebua

'Is my heritage to me like a hyena's lair? Go assemble all the wild beasts, bring them to devour.' -

Jeremiah 12:09

Thus, circumstance has compelled me to tell you, you know jack-shit about hyenas, dear. This, for instance: hyena is not an animal, but an edge; where grief has its house, her whetted territories sing. The opposite of *pleasure* is not *pain.* Hyena does not dig the dead from their graves, but where bodies meet the sun half-way, she is the war's mute treasurer; she has carried away our loss in moist parcels, with an extremity of tenderness. Draw around a sleeping dog with chalk. Turn away and count to ten. Hyena will rise. Patroness of feral misgivings. Her several habitats are as follows: Lebanon, Versailles, the Falls Road, Honour Oak after a storm. That which you call her *pelt*, her overalls; that which you call her *mane*, her crown. Tuppenny crones prefer the sleek indifference of felines. Hyena is her own raving spectrum, mascot of ruder perversions. It is a militant witch indeed who rides the long night into Rorschach, nose buried in her sweating neck. In the mid-nineteen-seventies radical lesbian separatists hoisted her face like a flag over pool halls and dive bars. In the late-nineteen-nineties her loping form was sighted in a comet's spitting tail. It is said that if you see a hyena in your dreams, you will die a violent death. This is true. However, hyena is not *harbinger*, but *prophet*. Some people simply will not be told. In Guadalupe her image appeared within a Black Mission fig, and similar visions have been reported in the South Hebron hills near Susiya. To find the image of hyena in a piece of fruit is to be brought not luck, but fortitude. Within the troublant ecologies of loss, hyena is the undisputed *Mater Lachrymarum*, or *Third Mother*. Her signature manoeuvre is the planchette, sharp-silhouetted corsair crossing any bucking sea. The night revolves around her, and didn't I tell you that all hyenas are female? That is, all hyenas are pirates. Hyena, our funerary renegade, is a poltergeist in a hair shirt. Where taxonomists say the hyena is closer to the cat than the dog, it is our stated position that hyena is closer to a Baby Grand piano, to an Acme safe in free-fall, to a typewriter thrown from a hotel window. And dearest, hyena is nearly extinct. To become a hyena is to live without captains or champions, to tarry packless in dangerous places: sectarian rec grounds, hospital corridors. Hyenas love well, but not often. There's a fine line between *woo* and *woe,* what she'd do to impress you, a million pitchy costumes. Hyenas are prized for

the aphrodisiac qualities of their hindsight. Men have
been grinding their bones to powder for centuries. Poor
fools. Hyena's power is not in her marrow but in the near
miraculous knack of her cherishing. She has been known to
sit vigil for eight-hundred years. Hyenas have no proverbs
only poetry. That which you cruelly describe as *howling* is,
in point of fact, the end of a song you persist in mishearing.
Blatant wassail, karaoke. How sorrow is ground like a coarse
blue lens.

Hyena! Jackal! Dog!

Wild Talents

'...there is no man who is without the hyena-element in his composition, and there is no hyena that is not at least rudimentarily human...' - Charles Hoy Fort

on the day of your death i became a striped
hyena. hysteria's lank technician, cursorial
man-eater, witch's mount. i ran, feliform punk
with my mane of stale thistles, over primrose
hill, across blackheath, to gnaw the shinbones
of monuments. dragging my afflicted eye
through the cagey *manors* of frasers
and richardsons, each lesser kray. london's
twitchy slang bloomed under me. i was not
afraid. animal, abandoned to its instincts,
slouching down the twisting vennel steps
to lick the yeast of my misdeeds. i tore your
bleakest manna into strips, left pennants
of its dark meat snagged on the late-victorian

railings. in cemeteries i scorned inscriptions,
wiped my hazy scent all over. *i* was the fur
atlas of my loss, and the yellow grass grew
sharp where it rubbed on me. your heart's
varmint. darling of the solvent park, weaving
the obstinate dusk into silent film. starry cuss,
i did not sleep, but lay, panting, on a raft
of trash: the serial bed-wetter's flammable
mattress, saturday magazines still in their
cellophane. empire, mine. my hackles in
the full flag of this failed state, flea-bit.
the day after your death, when they found
me, hoax-wraith white up road's wide
middle. i think i was running. i think
i'd been dreaming: i was the starkest
hound of my spirit. gargoyle against this
human bruise.

Hyena builds a bonny

From feuds and stalemates, all the fair weather democracies
of the heart. When I say *heart* I mean only the tetchy pulse
of the climate. I mean only our survival, a miracle of little
distinction. Hyena watched her husband's meat defrost for
hours, until it became a caravel, pink and awash on its own
melt tide. To be a hyena, an eruption in the level flesh, the
cavities and silhouettes beneath your observable world.
Hyena was hungry. *Keen* is a word that holds something
desperate and suggestive about language. The shrinking
missionary tedium of cities, around which walk the indigent
ghosts of all her doomed teachers. There is nobody left now.
Asked where she was when she *heard the news*, she can't
recall. She was going through the bins round the back of
Marks & Spencer's, or being called a *communist cock-wreck-
er* on the internet; she was *home*, with the priests winding
themselves up like racist cabbies, and little girls, gullible

and luminous, making her name into a skipping rhyme. Who knows? Who cares? It's all blah-blah, *kif-kif* now, innit? It's the Other One she thinks of in the night, the skinty whirr of his voice as he fraggled about at the front of the picket. Dysfunctional prefect, school-bully blazer open to the wheezing wet. It was summer. Hyena rolled up her human sleeves, and he saw her, and he knew her for a velvet leper like himself. What makes some of us hide in plain sight, while others commit to grievous loping through the static parks? Can anyone free the hyena in themselves and live? To be a hair-stickler, to sculpt your scarce weight into battlements, to be an armoured dog. Not *carnivore*, but *scavenger*. Her vegan teeth grew sharp on liquorice root. Mentors, plangent and sodden. Clever dicks who lead by their blighted examples. Hyena builds a bonny. Tired of her own tweedy scent. Tired of her body, a dull wool sleeve, trailing in a library. Pile up the practical chairs. The books. The chronically toxic copying toner. Injunctions, edicts, sound advice, everything must burn. In the world outside, men are fretting mutton, buying their council house, paying into their pension pots. Hyena doesn't care. To be convulsive and juvenile, to make of life one grimy boast. There is no one left to imitate. Tin soldiers with eyes like shit heirlooms. There are no mistakes to learn from now. Cipher of sleek foreboding. Hyena on her hind legs in a green silk skirt and paratrooper boots. Flashes a grin to camera, silently mugging, like Harpo fucking Marx.

Hyena in her human form attends a funeral

there was, of course, his mimsy girl: apt
witch with her spread of gossamer divinings.
not me. or again the *brilliant friend*, her dear
face caught like a wasp in a cobweb. boys
with staunch lusts mizzled into anecdote.
eminent dressers, all eyes drawn into
the orbit of their wardrobes. there were
smugglers of honey, doomed ones lost in
the errand of their jeopardy. i was not
afraid. beneath their clothes they're pink
like links of sausage. look away, look again.
in the albinising light before the storm, i'm
there, smelling of creosote and spent
pleasure. striped sardonicus, writhing
in the grim heat of my rictus genes. i am
always there, jawjacked and bleakly
glitching. a baddy's cackle. the zip

on a vamper's dress drawn down
at zinging speed. my laugh. my lips
ripped back to their sateen lining. this
deviant seam. wind-change artist,
neither cat nor dog. but oh, i've hung
his name from my mouth in reddest
shreds. this tongue a flag i've flown
from mildewed ramparts. sweet girls he
had, who filed their teeth and took their
meds. and me, convulsing and whooping
without joy. look again, look away. look
again. i have turned my face to the wall.

The striped hyena's laugh

You're wrong, of course. It does exist. Hyena deals in *se-crets*, not in *spectacles*; won't show it to just anyone. You do not know what laughter is. The dream of a forest, reduced to fidgets and to fragrance, a long giddy falsetto stunt, the *gimme* motto of her colleagues. No. Hyena's laugh is a fisher of limits, will twist her honeyed energies towards the keenest edge. The feculent mouth, ploughed up. You mistake the gekkering of telemarketers, all those toothy musketeers, for laugher. What you call *laughter* is the frictionless pidgin of amateurs; it is ordered online, and it ships worldwide, in sealed air baggies, stagnant and extrovert. Hyena's laugh is the night condescend inside a hard blue marble. Yours is maverick toad-work; a minister of state smarming in a headlock. It is a trick stomach, the gimmicked throat. Hyena laughs but rarely. Her laughter is not summoned. It is swift and mute as vengeance, never conjured up, by pratfall, cocktail, pungent junglebud; by ridicule or tickle. Her laughter is nocturnal, skunk bulk gliding through underground cities, toting its prole melody. Hyena's laugh is not the rubberised whoopee of expelled air. It is a sudden glitch in her sloping form as she dips beneath the yardarm. It is often silent. A kind of *presto!* A kind of splayed *cadabra!* In its sudden flux she has been known to turn textile, become a rush mat flattened out for welcome. It has its citric hiss, its cynic frailty, dark adjuncts, but most of all it is a kind of brackish hymn sung under the breath. No, it is not a chorus for skeletons and predators. It does not belong to your world of crocks and spoils, the tottering succour of cities, arts council funding. It is not a meat prescription, a kind of gargoyle propaganda. It is a subtle electricity, and you are its object. Like history, its origin is asking. Hyena will never laugh *for* you, will let out her luscious amen to the wind alone. You do not know what laughter is. Hysterical triage, the gremlin usury of femmy blondes: snob-music, ligging a drink. Oh no, A laugh is a windfall of wild peaches. A wayward nature tuned toward mercy.

Hyena tidings, with fuchsia

ribbed in vain weather. cerecloth sky. *the spring*
won't chase this sickness from the parks, he said.
and fuchsias' tactless finery, an ache under my
tongue. *homeland,* i want your lochs and sects,
your bony, hobbled ancestry. red ecstasy of risk,
this lockjaw congregation, this profanity of flowers.
hyena never understood how pain makes people
passive. she is *so* full and bright, could glow
these slums to thunder, shake the houses all
apart. there are women in this town, blown
about like grave dollies. hyena's next door
neighbour, a cemetery's paper matriarch.
stuff her mouth with marigolds. her grief
a grimacing lethargy. *pikey* opens up
her folded face by the corners of its fortune.

by *pikey* she means *hyena.*
there are women in this town, holding the last
of the soap in their pasteurised hands. oh cacao,
oh cardamom. i could clean the world with
just two wizened limes, hyena says. i could
drink the world, like one long fatalist mojito.
homeland, i want your famines and your
jeopardies. you are scarlett o' hara and god
is your witness: you will live through this,
and when it is over, you'll never go hungry
again. no, nor any of your folk. you are
scarlett o' hara as a brilliant dog. that is,
a hyena. spindly and gilded, your ormolu
body polished to a deathwish waste
of golden streamers, storm my dirty
hooded bloodline, make me maypole – oh!
spring's herald, my chronic skin
a kite for catching air. hyena says, in her
dreams she steps out of herself like saint
bartholomew, flayed. she says her skin
is a locked room. she says she is
saint bartholomew's statue, men
all gathered marvelling its fascist
meltweight. she says, she says. she
works her tongue to smudge in saying.
hyena is fur on the inside. soft-footed

geographies of *body* picked apart
to nude misrule. and leave her open to
the weather. and leave her following
buttery crumbs to the witch's oven.
and leave her to the speechless pagan
spite of empty places. *homeland.* there
is no home. there is no land. the ogham
of self harm. the depthless, tremulous
red of the sea, a fuchsia's antic mourning.
say, *we used to go gathering.* say, *this is
a yearnful music.* say, *cold has caught
the wings of birds; season of ice – these
are my tidings.*

Hyena! Jackal! Dog!

Hyena!, 38

Our bodies, mere diagrams of coming splendours: meno-
pausal death-pledge, luminous errancy of cells. I have been
in prison. Misrule in the rapturing networks. Odes of for-
getful intent. Blood runs its slow amok, triumphal, even.
All of their wagering woes, the desperate. We will ossify or
spawn. Neither ornaments nor monoliths. We've only been
glimpsed from the neck up for months. I have become a
chaste stone head, revoking my pronouns in airless rooms.
Listen. I listen, alone, at night, to my own whimpering reser-
voirs. To be irrational and ravishing, one time, a preferential
flirt. But no: with my suedehead, my grim misgendered dis-
position, I am the set-faced siren of aggro: Gloria Swanson
via Richard Allen. Poets, with your prizes and your cliques,
your institutional metaphors, all you curating angels, I'll
nick your Achilles yet. Or else desist, capitulate. I too have
my gods of dark dissuasion, entropy's precipice: *feed.* I don't

miss London. On days such as this the streets are torpor and attrition. Summer, its verdant pejorative: thistles, sorrels, worts and banes, the birds in their counterfeit imabs, *lilting.* The body cannot bare such heat. We come, with our bellyful of flimsy yearnings, with our bellies full of belly. The heart, in all its self-proclaimed acuteness, must surely out, give out. Is a silver star like a sheriff's badge. Is the law's tacit occulta, a hidden malformation at the root. I have been in prison. The scrappy algebra of unemployment, piece-work, reinventing enmity all the live-long day. In the Kingdom of the Poem there are no heroes, only despots. You catalysts, you clockers-on, and me, I'm just as bad. Our bodies are the calendar, the cell, the altar, and the vigil. Light candles to precarity, to all the day-glo alchemies of capital, the *things* we will become. No appraisal, only energy. A woman is this *coquille* encore prized from sleep to sex forever. Type your own name into Twitter. The sheet asserts its stains. The body, double-tongued, how muscles have a memory, how I could keep this up all day, this mirthless lyric riffing. Recursive, cursive grunt and flux. To be quenched. Or to live off light, have done with reckless slaking, live *inside* the lightbulb. To deign, to dare, to be more than the sweat of our retention, the fallopian headlong, picking a scab like a geisha's mouth. To breed more tender expectations, to be a brazen idol, popped under the tongue. Garishly equipped, in a kind of morbid cosplay with my myself, I'm amplified against the

Hyena! Jackal! Dog!

sun, against these cornucopias of bollock-rending smut. Virginity's golden tyrant. Planted by ancestors: here, right here.

Hyena! Jackal! Dog!

Hyena! outro rockstar rant

Gonna get the girl, gonna kill the baddies, and save the entire planet – Pop
Will Eat Itself

sometimes the wound is a weapon.
yeah!
sometimes the weapon is a wound.
my name with an exclamation point.
still-life with bullshit embargo.
the hashtags of corporate hygiene,
go fuck yourselves. i cut my teeth
in a plague year, bitches. i'm done
with your choric conniving, poetry:
sausage-fleisch and choleric, and get
your ape hands off of me, touchy feely
in the groupthink of your grief.
in the aether, on the edges: Hyena!
this year's *thing* is the nepotist's tightrope,
cut by some scorpion upstart. Hyena!
is the forward of all doom, a cocaine

emoji, a fur rubik's, voluptuary renegade.
you don't see her coming because
she is old. look again, clock
the hag mouth rubied up all baby jane?
that's your blood, poetry. if you
even have blood, poetry. if you're not
a face painted on an egg.
there's this song in her head.
she wrote it. it doesn't exist. in another
life there were groupies, so many plastic
gimme babies, and they wanted her
like some leather disease. or not. in
truth Hyena! traced the weeping career
of a candle alone, and shunned a face
all glammy oxides, platinum
and platinumest bruise, a severe cheek
turned to sequins. wanted to be pure;
to leave them aghast with a cold desire.
her and her sued-head, her and her joan
of arc pudding-bowl. her and her
terrible teeth!
hearts trade their petty syrup
monopolies: *who are you, Hyena!?*
where are you from? break a word into
prikaza, spit and colour. how the mouth
fills up with a false confession, how

the mouth fills up with motifs and with
sand. go fuck yourselves. your poem is
a dick-pic, your poem is a dna profile,
worked up from a single pubic hair.
i'm done with you. Hyena! is done
with you. got the memo at thirteen:
you're a girl, forget it. nothing but
gyrating, gaga, through a spancelled
twilight, preening and upholstered
in eyes and hands and eyes. nothing
but a bathtub suicide and a revised
history. Hyena! is plath gone enfield.
Hyena! is the sexless boggart
of a manchester slum clearance.
is a hobnailed squatter nailing his
unabomb thesis to the door
of your frigging starbucks. Hyena!
is also your androgynous moon-
face with his doctrine of soft
afflictions. they tried to tell Hyena!
who she was: a fleshy chevron
at the exit marked *sex!* billowing
and earnest in a wheat field,
patronised on late shows
by renegade jazz fiends. jesus wept!
they said: *you're your own art*, hot-

head and cherry bomb, or –
you're nothing. Hyena! isn't
pretty. she needs the medicinal hinge
of a word, joining her to her own
skin by the skin of a felty verb;
a space for all her *vibes* and *poses*.
there's this song in her head. or
there was. verminous flirt in studs
and spikes, and the gig is a stick-em-
up dumb show, u.v light eats your
partial recall. in another life, pock-
marked enthusiasts, pawing her;
sheepy faces shuddering their
phantom pronouns. Hyena! is
a queer messiah, here to *hex*
the patriarchy. by which she
means you, poetry. the patriarchy
is a giant comedy foot, has its own
spotlit alcove at the reykjavik
penis musem, is eating taco fucking
bell off a ten thousand dollar
table, is writing *yass queen* in
piss in the snow, thinks it can
sell you back to you. bitch, please,
i shed my skin in an acid year.

by which i mean my skin is acid.
by which i mean my words erode
the mouth that shapes them. listen,
instagram is a patient feedback form.
nobody gives a shit about
your *brand.* Hyena! turns her holy
silhouette to hands. holds her own
words out to you. she is offering
or aiming, repents the capsized sun,
is tearing her hair in mortician's drag.
sometimes the wound is a weapon.
yeah!
sometimes the weapon is a wound.
wanted this space to gather her limp
minutes into standstill, to make room
for her, the misfit's misfit. never mind
eileen myles or patti smith. Hyena!
is with ma rainey singing *prove it*
on me in a nightclub lounge. Hyena!
is for aversion and brawl on a deadpan
soho street in 1996. no more innuendo,
the teetering cairns of tedious *entendre.*
we are all Hyena! and we are done with
you – you're ours now, yes every slickly
swooning line...

Hyena! Jackal! Dog!

Hyena commitments

Hyena is not *political,* merely bruised. Wearied, condemned
in absentia. *He who has iron has bread.* No, my dear. He
who has iron has language. We saw them at work, erecting
argots to posterity. Nights of detour, sullen irrepair, in a city
of plinths, in a city of scapegoat masonry. On days made
samey with heat, how the body sizzles. Hyena has not slept,
wresting words of *love* from her gloaming tongue. Rapists in
a waking dream. Skin fades, organised into roaring militias.
Onslaught of pornography. *Not* political. Speak softly into the
wind against all the precision mischief of capital. World of
repeals and breaches, of penny-ante whistle-blow, drooping
through the days. *I do not feel essential*, the worker says, *but
sacrificial.* After all, they speak this ultimatum into shambles
weekly. A woman is something even less than sacrifice: a
series of banal ablutions, a liar's oath sworn on a stack of
bibles. Hyena is a fur harangue ran mad through these meth-

ane fields. Lethal and ignorant, the bourgeois fear of crowds. Book reviews, raptures of discernment in the Guardian, she hates. Fashion's furtive tiptoe through these quarantines, untenable thread count for minimum wage. Our lady of Retail. Our paragons of chic couture. Catechists of Instagram. A hyena is not *political.* is the fog at the back of the throat, not nearly a word, a syndrome. Is the ragged seam between language and amnesia. A fire in a wig factory. You, malingerers on Twitter. Where Sarah Vine is a witch-finder's finger. Where Cumming's head is a poison gourd. Don't you wish you could burn it all down? Don't you wish your girlfriend was hot like us? From houses, mumbled into borough as an afterthought. Sink estates disgorging their grot-persuasions. Land of retributions, dialects, a dealer's revenant ministry. Don't touch us, we will fly apart like a swollen murmur of birds. Hope and glory. Groped and horny. Hyena, raising an eyebrow with difficult languor. Umbrage, courtly displeasure, an opera of awkwardness, touching in gloves. You, veterans of pleasure getting silkily signified, don't you wish you could burn it all down? Let your anger cohere into heresy? Hyena didn't etiquette. Hyena didn't Marxist summer school. Hyena didn't Poetry London. Hyena didn't Bloodaxe. Hyena wasn't sexing her pedantry for boys and boys and boys, shining her pout like an empire apple. Women are purgatory and subterfuge, an *as if* protest, melancholy yearning. This is *not* political. Politics requires a centre, we have an edge,

Hyena! Jackal! Dog!

are an edge, how an edge is a commons, compassionate and
teetering. There will be no embraces. You, who claim to be
sick of a skunky crush in suburbs. Don't you wish? Don't you
wish wishing were a pure thirst, a means to an end, a raving
salvage in itself? Don't you wish we were more than a motto,
a moist eye rolled toward utopia, utopia as theme-park,
utopia as gift shop? Hyena is not *political*. Who has no iron,
who has no bread, who will unscrew the inscriptions from
statues. Land of deficit and bawling vendetta, the grimly
expert. Johnson's few deft crudities, Trump rigging famine
in his favour. This is politics, a kind of anti-life. The smiles
of racist comics, amused by their own jokes. Hyena has no
dogma only appetites. Where women become cutting tools.
The moment is now, whenever now is.

Hyena! Jackal! Dog!

I will learn to be more brazen

hyena says, rubbing her eyes until her waking
rings true. brazen is as brazen slides the gorgeous
stain inside the mouth. hyena walks into a room
like a heron in a koi pond. there are your bony,
mouldy gods; there are the women, offering up
their cloudy sighs when stepped on – puffball
fungus all. hyena had a friend, now the friend
is retaining water and talking up the dharma
of a cupped tit: babies. give her the glass slipper
of a contraceptive coil any day. no offence. well,
some offence. well, all the offence you can eat
if you must. the doctor told hyena there was
nothing they could do. he put his hand up her.
he pulled her about like a ship's cook peeling
a potato. hyena wanted the pain to stop –
flawed and floored – just cut the bad bit out.

but no, it's *no can do*, and *what if you want
kids one day*, and *how does your husband
feel*? hyena will learn to say that he is not
the one with a mediaeval jousting tournament
in his reproductive crawlspace, so how would
she know, and why would she care, and why
should it make any difference to you? if a baby
is a blessing or a miracle, then hyena is a what?
a blasphemy, a curse. she will learn to be more
brazen. she won't sit home all day, rake leaves
against ruin, picking the bone of perfection to
a witch's finger. she won't bite her nails, cast
lots for a creosote tea in the shit cafe. she will
not take a swilling stand beside the urns of dingy
brew, and turn her face to the wall in crowds,
and people will not say of her that her voice
is the murky mirror of her own self-hatred.
her voice, pared down with an emory board,
an anglofile. ha-ha-ha. she can almost see
herself in red. she is moving with the furies
in precise circles, taking slow sardana steps,
reaping the corn with the hem of her skirt,
using the wet silk edge as a scythe. her feet
will foment dances, trample grapes. she might.
and no longer lie awake, burning with a sullen
fervour, eyes on the artext, breathing asbestos.

a fierce heat will flow through her fingers.
when she meets a swan maiden she will spit,
and there will grow a heart-shaped swimming
pool. hyena will learn to be more brazen,
have a male voice choir comb her mane
until it gleams with the posthumous lustre
of a victorian daguerreotype: the misty dead
propped up in their chairs. oh, she will be
flagrant. she will have cupboards full
of cordials, the sacristy bursting with candies.
a real witch. a prairie pyro inflamed by the long
dark night. she will tie the orchard to the tail
of a kite and let it go. she wants you good
and thirsty, ready to make sacrifices, spooked
by fire. on the day of her rebirth she will hold
a bal masque where everyone must come
dressed as their own worst fears: the eliot
long list, dying alone, postal voters, etc.
hyena will come as the thin white line between
savour and decipher; a mundane chill that will
not suit her coat, her mood. her most fulsome
costume is herself, wrapped in the stealth
of strong gauze. listen, you, who pity her,
she wouldn't be you for all the lithe republics
of a country saying. these, her nimble, quickened
sounds: exalted thoughts, learning how to swim.

Hyena! Jackal! Dog!

Hyena Q&A

Q: And what's it *like* being a hyena?

A: It is like withdrawal, trembling its traces all across the
splendid belly of the night. It is ecstatic and mechanical,
a kind of sanguinary prickling, to be made spectral with
adrenaline, to stream raw light through your fibre optic
veins. It is holding the ice of his name in my mouth until it
cools. Until, I mean, it thaws.

Q: How has being a hyena affected your employment
prospects?

A: Imagine having a clubfoot. Except it isn't your foot, it's your whole body. Imagine a woman's face eaten away by radiation. That's how people look at you, a cheesy fifties pinup, her thighs tempered with ugly ragged holes.

Q: But *do* you work?

A: I practice walking upright. I type with a hollow wand between my teeth, a tango-dancer's wilting rose.

Q: Have hyenas many friends?

A: Spotted hyenas travel in packs, like non-league football supporters. A strand wolf is rarer, androgynous thicket, a sweating maze of hair. A strand wolf forms a band in college, is sad, stratospheric and doomed, likes to be looked at, never touched. The striped hyena is *not* musical, will wear a big-ass garland of garlic bulbs to keep at bay all vampires.

Q: Vampires?

A: The opposite of *hyena* is not *human.* The opposite of *hyena* is *vampire.*

Q: Does a hyena ever take a lover?

A: *Thistles* are not *thorns.* There is no *thorn soup*, just as there is no *hyena love.* Sex is a wet ghost, solicitous and pitiful, his thin mouth open like the meekest wound. There was a *sweetheart* once, exemplary gelatine, the sugared whorls of her haunches dissolved in milky tea.

Q: What kind of answer is that?

A: What would you have me say? There were dauntless boys, doubly gone, and a girl who spoke in maudlin strophes the briny savour of *suicide.* A hyena bears her own irreparable juju. A hyena is both the Jonah and the boat.

Q: Are you trying to tell me something?

A: Yes, like Sappho.

Q: Are *all* hyenas lesbians?

A: Some people have a way of saying *lesbian,* like a foot being stamped at a children's party. Your eyes are the most indiscriminate blue, like the faulty jizzing flames of an electrical fire. I do not desire you. I do not desire. Neither grunt and thrust nor coax and yearn. Picture Valerie Solanas swooning in a field of wheat. You can't, can you? There is no *thorn wine* either.

Q: Does a hyena know when she will die?

A: Yes, in the grime of twilight, fermenting a requiem among the rotten apples. They will build a shrine to me beside Camden Canal, but it will be inaccessible except by kayak. On the third day of my death, I will perform my first miracle.

Q: Does it bother you that you are such a tiresome person?

A: On my way here a line of gaunt yellow flowers, my crude little comrades, who fizz with wiry life. Do they give a shit that people think they're weeds?

Q: But are you *really* a hyena?

A: I have rubbed myself along the surface of the world. Extinction is a coal sewn into my belly. I put it there on purpose. A hyena is a punch-line in search of a joke.

Jackal!

Hyena! **Jackal!** Dog!

To live on dread

my mind is a fucking scorpion orgy, coerced into cartwheel
by lack of sleep. sleazes and dealers for days, bruv. be
afraid. *be very, very afraid.* on the stroke of ten, then london
becomes a flash-mob made of malevolent exes, upskirting
clerks in novelty ties, gym bunnies picking the disney
princess that best represents them. it's friday night, and
the gang's all here, and you should make peace with your
god. on the tram to new addington, dickwit contingents
are lisping their colony motto, fontanels softened by a
politician's kiss: *white pride! white power!* the flower of
english manhood. babydoll dresses are heading to mass
karaoke with extra prosecco, to chicken wing and bingo
hall, or slumped on the night bus to nowhere. a cut-price
penal hell no traveller returns from. be afraid. *be very, very
afraid.* fear is a chemical fetish here, an echo, a headrush,
an apt dread of numbers; a rusty nail and a tabooed lust.
my mind is a clock with a fire-gilded face. attention's

golden deficit is strained, is stretched, has been beset by
the divil in diverse shapes. and worse. the man who grabs
at my pussy in parking garages. racehate and faceache
and gollywog jam. i don't want to go back. mooncalves in
shell-suits peddling cretinous kiddiefuck. the national front
horny on shore-leave, brutalist stag-do, twisting my arm
'til it cracks. i fear the grotesque english real, perturbed in
my porcel, degenerate bones. on the news is an april fool
made flesh: competitive error, compulsive lie. pestilence
and penetration. hanna-barbarians all. there's a headwound
like a rooster's comb, middle-class courtesans stalled in a
motorcade, wet links of shit falling out of a dog, a flickknife
with my name on it. i've polished my mind like a five-
pointed star and lived inside my most absolute name in
a vegan extremist kingdom of one. a bare-hard season,
clutching my keys. social media is a tedious monologue of
self-care. life-coach mantra, spastic at yoga, unexceptional
text-event where no one is saved. friday night, and police
are battening down their collective brain-death, coming for
us, breathing through their mouths. i live within the poem
like some straight-edge walter mitty, indicate my fussy hurt
in airless rooms where daylight is entangled or revised.
poetry's a sow's ear, whispered into service. we're working
out our unmutual purpose, dread and i. my most conducive
doom. what is missing is absent on purpose, the regular hole
in a chinese coin

On taking leave

london, my dirt baptism.
where sweat settles into jelly.
where i am a hollow chocolate
rabbit, a bond girl dipped in gold,
for you. london, your moneyed
immersions. your eyes like belly-
dancers' jewels. disney supremacist.
a bloodied shovel, turning greedy
oncers into loam. you are a serial
killer's scrapbook, a million
weathergirl mutilations.
the suckling cabaret of sex
and junk. we cross the bridge,
and i sink back into your hurt
perfume. london, you stink
like a whore on expenses.

you're a cleaver in a tux, a jilted
crybaby psychopath with cash
to burn. it's getting
late. london, you ate the moon
through all her phases, down
to a pair of slim gold croissants.
as above, so below. and suicide
ushers the acetate thames.
i am sick of your formalist
handiwork: women in
textile slings, stretched out.
my own face, super-
imposed on a stack of wooden
serving bowls. money,
with its cunning freight of lusts.
to make these desires my own.
to mistake window displays
for the satiny fuck-pad interiors
of the skull. to mistake display
windows for antique mirrors.
london, my teeth are pink
and i am not buying. a ponzi-
hag, your brain a green olive,
disintegrating in vermouth.
i am not buying. your bigotries

mortised into law. signed,
then countersigned, then glyphed
onto party political hoardings.
i cannot be here. loved you
like a cosh, like a combination
monocle-and-speculum,
like the ash-dessert of my grief.
through all the high-rise
succorscapes of addicts, bandy
lanes of misbegotten bric-a-brac,
camden squats coming apart
at their edwardian pilasters.
i loved you, wasting another sunrise
on the shrunken or the stumbling
umbra of our former selves.
at the top of the horse hospital
drinking chicory shit to
the coarse ozone
of another sunday morning.
i had loved you like the scissors
in my thigh; the way i always
have to pass my hand through
candle flame. london, lord
of motormouthed zeitgeists,
high priestess of distractions,

marzipan harangues. even i
would breathe again. you're a bad
mother, a slapstick camp, a lipstick
smear, a wrist weighed down by
trinkets, screaming *no*
more wire hangers! you're a shit
kingdom of suction and plunge,
and you've killed all those
who loved you best. whip your latte
smooth-talk into wormwood, london.
a chorus of matriarchs, ruined
by gin. at the hour in which all
cocktails become nail bombs, you
are playing statues in a sewn coat
of meat, in feathers of envy, wiping
your mouth on the back of your
hand, eating you hand, being *all*
mouth. yes, i *lived by the river,* knew
your several moods of waltz and brawl.
oh, knots and crosses. oh, leather
enzyme. once, your bony zealot.
london. *rattenkönig*, calqued
into english, the sticky stuff by
which we're bound. cried for your
fascist glitter, once. but now

there's a sky inside of me, wider
the chimneys, wants to stretch
its love – in birds.

Hyena! **Jackal!** Dog!

Dispatches from the Bleach Year

instead of poets, what?

the exit fictions of refugees. night's i'd dynamite these sties. police, who come to anglicise our cherub faces dead. greasy daub of form against the glass. an ugliness surpassing poetry at all. a walk where houses heckle me, belabour paper rainbows. children who draw around children in chalk. my stalker, wearing his obsession like an apron. presidents. heroes, a sword that exceeds the arm that holds it. four a.m., its oaths of early fire. inscrutable republics of contagion. the caterpillar tongues with shit between their treads. instead of poets self-made millionaires prolix on oxycontin and holocaust denial screaming *don't you know who i am*?!?! to an empty airport. the bollix of birdsong, barking dogs. music of epiphany and tinnitus, the varmit hyperbole of hip-hop. the bland caucasian warble of a late nineties girl band. a nurse like a consummate phoenix rising from a cup of cold black coffee, her tongue's true substance is not meat but emergency. a suspension of parking, anti-climb spikes on the wall of a church. my stalker, trimming skeletons from paper, a version of me he will fold up for later, a stripped proposal of bone, a guinea indulgence waiting for flame. gadgets that replace the hands that held them. balconies, dandling their dark rebuke in broken bikes and bunting. a red cross on a white field, bedsheet cut in queasy quarters, offered up with holes and stains. ghosts, scrawny in their haunting, between the laundrette and the takeaway. couples in the comic rock opera of their rowing. a woman's face in fridge magnets rearranged. instead of poets climates and surfaces. women in floral headscarves cleaning tombstones in churchyards, a peanut gallery of the dead. infirmity and irredemption, convalescent plasmas. sunsets that outstrip their facebook feeds. terror, poking through the thin venetian slats of our vanity. the skunk humidity of stairwells, barely breathing in, the bins not emptied. a social-distancing quadrille in carparks. trump's detergent fault. foxes, capsized and copulating on liverish mornings run to weeds. the puny allure of suicide or heroin, letting go. snails as bright as glowing coals on my run in the rain. my stalker, stretching his vagabond's sangfroid into tedious *i told you sos* and how do you like me nows. a passive, clammy modesty. failure. phantom fucking plum suckers, shepherding a seemly phrase across the threshold of their sherries. nostalgia: a two-man tent put up indoors. the childish spasm of a hand against a hand. provocateur of blossoms striking at the psychic skin of instagram. scrolling my own face with dirty, spatulate aggression long into the wee small hours of my our collective irrelevance. cover versions of songs that weren't that great to begin with. politicos, verbose, opaque, afloat on error. reproach, disclosure, a landscape wearing sea-marsh like a mercy. frigate birds flailing their bitch-slap sorceries. black wings reaping the salt air clean above dry-docked cruisers. a coffin like a steinway. a flick-knife wielded against wanting. a reef of unsigned plaster casts in the grotto light of a & e. allegro confectioners, spilling their sanitised baggies from glove boxes. the metallic thirst of monday. menace, hiatus. the eye's briefest limerick wink. the lushy dynamo of sex. women in the eerie liniments of addiction poncing a quid to *feed the meter*. meter's bogus meadows. insipid nimble fingers playing girls just wanna have fun on a harpsichord. instead of poets the suction of a blank cheque upon a loosened bowel. journalists. men braiding the coarse mane of history into biddable plaits with the present. factories for tact, the salmon farms of giddy commonplace: this too will pass... it will be alright... the shunned, the judged, the prettily monstered, publicly shamed, a hundred thousand faces, dissolute in liquid going *noooo!!!* inexpert makeup of girls who wouldn't dare, the stowaways, the hoaxes, the stylers out of a porcelain whimsy on twitter in an artificial, economic gloaming. offspring sprouting like mushrooms in a cupboard. my bare neck ecstatic with heirlooms, buoyed by gold.

haircut with ungracious fervour. nude matrons streaking to escape. instead of poets a st augustine of echoes. the bleach inside inside. carrying my own slack belly like a cloth bag full of clothes-pegs. idolatry in unemployment. trump, the plectrum of his policy picking a tune in idiot time. a frigid civil music. lungs becoming difficult geodes. daily briefings. foremost oriflamme affront to reason. oracles of microsoft and solitaire. to burst, into flames. to burst into tears. r said *refrain* is to hold back, and to go on again, again. said *griot*, tells a story. *griotte* tells the slick morello cherry flesh. instead of poets a certain sweetness in the ear. turning back the sea, drawing down the moon. as if we could. like words are where we come to rot. mutton gluttony of dogs. the new normal. like words are what we eat when we're pure heat, horrendous text, locust, lotus melancholy. when we don't want to think. fingernails sticking in the wall of a well. when we don't want to think anymore.

There is a hole

into which i'd wad
your reluctant presence.
dog-eared now, or *foxed*,
this orphan pose. *hang-*
dog, dog-tired, waspish:
metaphor's plangent
bestiary, its animal
remainders. call a fig
a fig, and a trough
a trough, why not?
manic pixie dream girl
trope at nearly forty's
really *sad.* a bulbous
wreck. depression's
croneish bent. the tedious
hokey-pokey of weight

loss, weight gain, weight
loss. there will be no
snow angels, indie mix-
tape, video spin-off,
respite. this chilly
teacup scene wants rid
of me, slip into quiet
nervosa, mutilation's
clichéd spite, the lyric's
mawkish dalliance.
sometimes i tell myself,
i might. the tongue
tickles its stock
of *could've been*
contenders' speeches,
lays them on
a shelf, untried. what
is the use? going on,
your own effort closes
over you like waves
of rolling credits. to
stop is to become a pair
of floured hands, sensible
shoes, a walking condition.
the nodes grow nerves

inside of me. i am inside-
out, and it hurts, and it hurts.
there is a hole.
bigger than the body.
seen from the peak
the plateau is a hole.
the eye is a hole
but doesn't know it.
a hole is a well
that has outlived
its water. i am trying
to tell you. that has
outlived its village.
that has outlived
its haunting, its
japanese cinema
schoolgirl drowning,
its horror stories,
freak accidents.
just a hole. there's
a hole. which is
the mouth, when you
get right down to it.
which was always
the page. poetry
is ted kaczynski
in a satin jumpsuit

and mary janes.
is an amateur terrorist.
ulrike meinhoff played
by natalie portman.
is raving weather-
report uselessness.
poetry is a hole and i
tried to swallow you,
a light lowered down
and i'm sorry now.
at the bottom
of the hole, more
holes, a dynasty
of zeroes. the mouth
in stroppy colloquy
and i'm trashing around
like a shark in a boat.

'Doleful'

'But wild beasts of the desert shall lie there; and their houses shall be full of doleful creatures; and owls shall dwell there, and satyrs shall dance there.' - Isaiah 13:21

without poetry, where will you go? what will you do?

frankly my dear. this strangeness set in motion. how a bad
year lands like small change being tossed. and i cried in
my one good coat on the train from the funeral. these days,
my reflection is an anecdote. not yet an allegory. war, and
lesser rumours. my neighbour nearly dead. but i hated her
anyway. mosquito peace, the high-pitched whine that signals
cease-fire. tense. and boris is a walking relapse. eyefucks the
armoured industries. raab bombs iraq. you couldn't make
this up. the national sap is rising. the mutant treyf of baby
names. i will wear asterisks to emphasise where on the
dolly the bad men touched me. i will levitate in eco-friendly
beam-me-up. i will float above the rich. intoning through the
thrice chewed cud of policy. i will not hear them. i deliver
groceries, manual and ministering, to pretend i am good.
to move with the logic of comic books. frame to frame. to

say to myself: *the law of nature* – like politics – *is collective and overwhelming* slithering. cabinet belly-toads, raving and spawning. world of hummingbirds and juggernauts. by which i mean flitting things, abruptly crushed. attention is a whip hand wallowing in air. is deferred, averted. blear and crack. when the old woman opens the door to me her face is beige with fear. napoleon oranges roll from their stainless paper folds across her floor. her fruit bowl overflows, garrulous with mangoes. cherries then, lacquered and aloof. she stoops and stretches, sucks her lip, selects a reliquary shelf. pale sanctuaries of aspic. sachets of pink curing-salt. and cayenne sickles, wound *and* tool. illusions spool from kilner jars. and in the sea change of their saccharine the apricots grow white and fall to dim apothecary musing. jug of must. imperative and pith, the grist of grape. wine's tenement girlhood soon forsook. gelatines and nitrates. whitefish, wasting into feathers. tins. slender bodies break apart like endive seeds. suspended, *not* preserved. singing, under her breath. her song is striving in five directions at once. to name but two: mermaid felicities, grammars of lapidary disgust. i do not trust her. here, with her heritage of grafts and crops, where she is queen, a sphinx amongst the pickles. eater of anthems. the rich, i'm told, are like this: chew only dust. jawing the mummified crusts of their vocab in damp ancestral burrows. when she speaks, her staunch cambric iambs stand up starched. when she says my name

it is the sound of cheap latex tearing. a stifled cough in a
grocer's queue. *gyppo*, acid-etched in glass. escaping her. to
be mere on the heath for an hour, wet right through. pale
insteps stamp my curse to ridicule, tread her reliquary hex
to chaff going *my magic's bigger than yours, nah-nah-nah.*
the notable moon. the debateable moon. as if all moons had
sided with her, with them. and i want to get england where it
lives. i want to drive my replica samurai sword through her
throne.

Hyena! **Jackal!** Dog!

Autumn fever

the mouth becomes a prarie. and the dog
has a look on his face, like al pacino, who
knows it was you, and it breaks his heart.
unnatural practices, candle wax, omens
and sonnets, these things the night contains.
love is the salt sewn among your symmetries.
everything is beautiful and nothing grows,
the houses in their gothic hunkering, plates
and their *modest proposals* of bacon
and eggs. fever's fahrenheit threnody keeps
screwing everything up. elopement
and pretense, the tender years in which
fools and their wallets are parted. trysts
and frisks, the policemen patting us to
absolution, just because. how he walked

into a room like a dancer hitting his mark.
all the small calibre woes. macho scenes
played out to pure spaghetti: tequila,
cigarillos, a reble in a bandolier. your
casablanca hourglass, a heart-shaped
pool where her heart should be. and mine.
i keep falling asleep, wake to the typical
dark of studios, murnau in the flailing
gloom of heligoland, a morbid barge
full of earth, a morbid barge containing
all the plot-twists of insomnia, the old
world courtesy of a gaping wound. i am
tired of my body, of the starlet's
allegorical charms, of her tedious
petulent smouldering. autumn unfolds,
is mellowly wrested from vegetable loins.
arrives in strips like dank cellulloid.
our cardinal squib, our meanest movie.

Hyena! **Jackal!** Dog!

The abjection industry

you sound so angry, what else?

the losses of estrangement. the losses of bereavement. the
stinging quick of nettles, rash against my calves. becoming
a doctor on friday. blowhard windfuck in the trees above
the silent park, calling with all his gimlet invective: *you're
shit, and you know you are.* hooligan swoop of the fields.
campions. keck. the slips and knots. how summer is a
pressure that builds behind the eyes. a spurting fist through
spring. dragging carrots out of the earth by their hair. my
run is the only time i'm left alive. furtive and ill-fitting thing,
this nervous sack of shock. adipose pathology of thumbs
and clumsy yearning. god, i miss r, his savant vowels, mood
of appalled insomnia, doom's melodious premonition: *i see
you, hyena, in the dark.* when he stuck his arm in a beehive
to come back gloved in honey. like all poets, except he wasn't
holding a piece of poached comb broken awkward at the
base, but the anglo-saxon word for *paring blade*, a tiny owlet

carved from jade. affliction, colossal and obvious, is all i
know to name. poets. their alchemies and protocols, pale as
condoms inflated with air. like language is a cod posterity,
shit for that. or the boy like a beardsly venus, zealous on
amphetamines, expounding. i've loved his limpid words,
but fuck him too. i want my friend. wasps hover in the
haze of his name. little spears. little *arrows of desire*. little
metaphors for my own projectile spite. when i sleep i picture
the whole world bittering through his cisterns, making him
shudder and creak. imagination's figment windfall. every
last word for the wrongness of things. whose only proverb
was a pause. to need that now. instead of poets. death's
glowing rosette pinned to words, to shit of which we best
not speak.

Boon companion

that i have my honeycomb strongholds too,
impossible penetralia. shall i compare you
to a milky stoat? my mucus suitor, sifting
near the heart. hair weight weaved in
the throat. shall i compare you to a badger's
bone erection? thin migratory needle,
slivering in me. all disfigured favour now.
gallicrow for fallow fields. flailed lapels,
a fiction of thread. autumn is a spectrum
of disquiet. a finite infamy, pin in
a bubo. the blister on a lip. you
are a straw plateau made meal. the apple's
malic sting. rodent declensions, softly.
winter's stingeing appetites are on their
way. the mirror is your grail and your

bruise. the sun sinks its teeth into
a broken leg, the plough's malefic: crock
and tuber, seam and sherd, and reliquary
yield, all dead things turned up. us too.
you've the grinning sickness now, make
dirty talk like a smirking toy. canescent
spectre of the laurels. farmyard dark
of treadles and of cleavers. crack,
like a greased teat in the cold. show me
a midden and i will skim you the world
from its watery depths. who are you to
talk of *love?* who fucked the susceptible
chestnuts into blight. kingdom
of wimping benevolence. you cut
up my clothes with lambing's
six-week shears too late. a *v* of geese
slain in flight. the geas i lay. geist
you rouse to charm school in a pesty
dream. but i'll have my honey-come
strongholds too, my castle keeps, my
ridding mien. keep your pastoral
appeasements. spring runs cold.
my chilling vein.

A break in the weather

even the dogs, distended with heat. i wanted rain.
women with their conscientious shopping washed
away. these mutant brides of hygiene, trending
and aerobic, who *tsk* my dirty boots in queues.
this mineral stutter. gardens stained with brute
occasion. chalk reproach. hedges choked with
bunting. england: a comic turn, drawing a string
of flags from his fly. rapture of hands. i wanted
rain. trampling the vintage of a sun-fucked face.
on days when days are graves. lack gravity or grace.
men, in the blank stare of their tatts, whose guts
are globes, whose biceps groan with empire.
anchors, roses, fragments of a fragrant name. rain.
to rinse this sickness, island ridicule from skin. this
city, where history exceeds its shadow. stall
and loop. audition the deadpan fault that feeds on

us. again, again. estates unspeak their skinner box
verbatim. smoke. and flame. conditioned
and engulfed. we are. i wanted rain to put these
civic fevers out. they're burning still. in vicious
figment cinders, still. my friend, to tread your
empty name to echo. to write the slant exception
of your name on dirty walls. the rain would wash
this too. and our illuminated wasteland: the futile,
sovereign portraits of our martyrs: bishops,
pricks and pawns. and you. any name to sanctify
a scene of threshing hurt. tread these borders,
boards, you walk abroad like thespy ghosts.
could cast your emanated arms in wax this
night. christ's face in the grain of the kitchen
table. his imprint in the splinters. rain. to dress you
in this deluge too, and all our mob, their masochist
vulgarities, in chains and chains and chains. cats,
made manx with mutilation, maimed like saints,
they spray their sympathetic wounds on everything.
i wanted rain. percussive stunt with thunder purge
the shape of me made minotaur and new. to flirt
my thrashing form through calendars and mazes,
prose. where others have been before. and i am
the turd emoji of trespass, an effluent refrain you'd
scoop from pools. i have written this poem before.

no, this poem was written without me: into the decimal
amber jots of a pit bull's eyes forever. into the garret
appetites of libertines, the somnolent garotte
of smack, mouths slack with musing, yielding in
their eyries to the pleasures of the spleen. and chains
and chains and chains. and rain. escape is begun by
betrayal. give me courage enough for that. to know
all flags are hoax, all names. to refute her slovenly
canticles, that *fine old woman,* who's lairy pastures'
rearing only weeds. she'd bind your bogmouth
shut with reeds. tell me, my friend, why i feel so
unclean. on the corner, some preacher spilling
wilful tight-lipped syruptone, his reflection warped
in windows. the fields have shed their shovels too,
and idiots are out there, begging brightness from
sky, the cryptic elegance of herons, cranes, the
chancy depth of rivers. i wanted rain. concentric
shocks that drive me inward toward you. something
clockwise breaking. covert and austere. england: rolling
up the sleeves of rumour, readies his ringmaster's whip.
god is a portable darkroom tonight. your image resolves
in a shallow chemical bath. a whisper arrives from
the outside world. the rain will come. canned laugh.
little white lies. promises, promises.

Hyena! **Jackal!** Dog!

Your wounds

grapes in a season of succulent exception,
wet with risk. horned gods of the garden
send withy wind and basket willow; atropine
and mallow, *possession vine*, jenny's perennial
creep. sleep is stuffed with all the wreckage
of return, the body with eventful tremor.
here, the golden coach regressed, a pumpkin's
totalled opulence. suggestions of spring in
asparagus tips, projectiles of your sullen lust.
circuits of belated dissipation. solanine
and rhizome, bring the whole house down.
you poison everything. orange windows
winking their afflictions as i walk. your
crooning cantabile is bile. magpies' prussic
chorus, wagging parliament of tongues.
i dread you now, the blood all vertigo

and fireball, with fuck all on the telly. to cry
most days. the trees will not bear fruit
or die – just like me. and something comes,
a storm across the scalp, the ash of all
your sallies. a face at the window: *vinegar
tom*, teething, weaned from a *witch's tit,*
this sudden snap. the terracotta pots are
coaxed to eunuch ruction. everything errant,
then fecund, then spoiled. grapes!
of a turncoat sweetness rot. on the sodden
ledge the bilious wicks wax ruin's seize.
you poison *every*thing, all the knit
and smithy of an autumn night; my own
image in the splitting mirror, hoaxed
and vexed. cayenne's fire in kilner jars,
its sickle-swords to rust. london skies,
stele of vultures. house a cuirass, closing
in. you got into the garden. you
got into the walls, into the water, worm
in an apple, weevil in a bag of flour.
i put down chemicals, but you are
obstinate, immune, and in at every window,
every pore and calquing your courtly wounds
like wings. drawing a crowd. long nights
skulking in the sorrels, plucking myrtle's
white unwitting. obsession's posy, *picked*

and culled. all i want, the chalky tread
of hills, bald chill from the lovely-dirty
sea. to be free. give me peace. but you are
in the aether, in the heather, in the other,
in the hedge, perturbing parma roses,
polishing discretion's selves, their little
cults and conjuries, your spools and sprouts
of woe. grapes of a strenuous savour, burst
between finger and thumb, become
their own elegy. your wounds burst too,
into costume, into song. come strumming
your wounds, inward over the thistle-field
and to my door, always mine, and any door.
please leave me be. you bring the blight.
in a bent tin bowl with your own severed
extremities.

His dream

of course i'm still awake, turning up the collar
of my john doe coat and contemplating. a kind
of idle dread, an aggravated fracture. midnight's
cynical liquorice airs, apathetic threat. dreams
i could do without: molten seethe of sated faults,
something *beetling* in me. the pitching hour:
left hands tying little knots in memory. hitch
and splice, and cinch and braid; the ligature,
the shackle. dull blades suddenly scimitar.
a boning knife in the brain's dark paunch.
these are earthworks were his eyes. men who
loosen their belts for butchery. men whose
pedant hieroglyphs are wounds and wounds
and wounds. i have torn my temperate thumbs,
holding my own eyelids down. but of course
i'm still awake. something to do with the birds,

full of throat and faint of heart. or caught
in a crackdaw's vectoring regard, sized up
and minutely loathed. against the light
a wingspan is a *red right hand*, is a man's hand
steeped in the reeking clothes of its kill. i
talk myself into my bad dreams: institutions
under bleak skeins of snow; father, standing
in the wrecked lozenge of a november shed,
his arms full of leaves and weeping. young
boys, stricken or venturing, through rain
in its bafflements, towns made miserable
with victory, towns that say *après moi, le
déluge* in distillery tones. night's i'll feel
my exile coarsen into banishment. night
is wearing its shirt transparent at the breast
where the heart bleeds through. i have not
slept since england. last week on the lock
it was christ in his grave-digger's duds.
as the water soaked up his shovel he swore
he made a bed for me in paradise. i *could*
drown, hugging all these homesick trinkets
in my hands; my pockets gorged on hobnailed
votives. residues and rumours; places, parents,
friends. he was barely there, his body a smudge
on a log-book page. his wiry latitudes worked
out wrong: he should not be here. a growl

at the back of a dog without the dog. how he
should not *be here, be here, be here,* till sun
sent tendons of light to hold the red room up.
his dream became my dream. of course i
haven't slept. turn the combination lock,
sibilant and fidgeting. quarry, penetrated
clay, corrugated gardens. the sky arrives
on fire again. to wake his dream, to dance
his wake.

Hyena! **Jackal!** Dog!

Father / figure

safe house / say / f-uh / house / fun / house / un-house /
wrecking ball brings hope to slum[1] / they said / and peter's
death / would glorify to god[2] / with arms outstretched / and
upside down / his hair / is in his eyes / his mouth / and on
the long arterial road[3] / playmates / raised / on catafalques
/ and chequered bread / *get under the bed*[4] / they said / you
wept / the bullet carries / seany's head / upon its back / a
hermit crab / this / is everything they promised us / and
less / the big / *adventure of high-rise living*[5] // men / drag

1) headline in the *l a times*, october 31ˢᵗ, 1993. subheading reads: "gunmen and criminals have
given way to trees and driveways in belfast's infamous divis flats.
2) divis being in the parish of st peter. st peter as in simon peter, or simeon if you really must.
and simeon being a martyr, and crucified upside-down. and simeon's death being said to bring
glory to god. in the gospel of john. i'm writing this for the benefit of your university heathens.

3) an arterial road. as in through the falls to andersonstown.as in therapeutic phlebotomy. as in
emergency exit.
4) everyone was screaming, though mainly agnes.
5) so said mister gerry fitt mp, the subject of many popular songs and rhymes. in the 1960s.
when the flats went up. fair play, though. he said *adventure.* he wasn't wrong.

ging their knuckles / across the middle / distance / men /
with tattooed dewlaps / goosebumped in bermuda shorts /
they fly / their stomachs at half-mast / to speak of your da
/ you close your eyes / his fist revisits / his errant son[6] //
martyn / in a meeting / fifteen minutes / and then / an old
argument climbs / into / the plushy cockpit / of your mouth
/ a list of words / you never want to / hear again / *objective
/ authorised / empowered*[7] / and seany's head / you said
/ the bullet *travelled* light / the bullet / *passing through*[8] /
this wreckage / is what fathers do // safe house / say / f-uh
/ house / no house / is safe / nursing a nursery fate / with
mattresses against / the window / *the truth / commission
/* somebody / *commissioned this truth*[9] / you said / some /
body / considers *the past / rather than ongoing events*[10] /

6) you read me this article. male unemployment is 22 percent in ulster, but in divis it's twice
that. 7 out of 10 heads of household are unemployed. that's the phrase they used: *heads of
household.* and therefore alcoholism.and therefore domestic violence, blah. he hit me so hard
one time my eye popped out of its socket.

7) the truth and reconciliation commission, it's role as outlined in hayner, pricilla: *unspeakable
truths: transitional justice and the challenge of truth commissions,* (routledge, 2010). where do
you get this stuff?

8) as it did with patrick rooney. first star to the left and straight on till morning. *passed through.*
i hate this phrase. it makes it seem clean and easy and casual.

9) because "official" history can't contain this. and because it's like at school. and father
michael doesn't want you to *say* sorry, he wants you to *be* sorry, and he thinks by *making* you
say, you'll be. but you won't.

10) because it isn't over. because it's never over. because it can't be over until every single one
of us is dead.

Hyena! **Jackal!** Dog!

but time present and time past / are present in time future[11]
/ and your suicide sings / in the undecided light / where
childhood / redoubles its hiccups / picking the dead / skin
/ from its feet // say / f-uh / house / martyn / we deal in
traces[12] / not in time / you're with me yet / i'll orbit my own
/ private / portion of storm / candidate / for this / or that / i
watch the world / satellite the eye / is fattened / on systems
/ cyst/ cateract and cloud and clod / and the whorled
ozone / sundered blue / the view from here / acquires the
logic / of distance / a blank page is god // oh, say / how do
houses speak / recycle their damage / into new resources[13]
/ resist / when i put on my books / commit / this forfeit
of allegiance / and when / the forfeit returns / with a
vengeance / in the morning / or / impelled towards sleep's
velvet spasm / all our dark interiors / exposed / it has never
not been now / divis is / combing the stones / from her feral
smile / bury you / invent fresh history / history exists / *to
punish the excessive / demands of its poets*[14]/ ollam / i covet

---

11) you're paraphrasing. mr t. s. eliot, redoubtable fascist-sympathiser, from *burnt norton*,
1935. didn't know i knew that, did you? death is a very modernist impulse.
12) trace is that which is outside time—chronological time, time as it is tracked by official
historical record—and yet immanent to it as disjointing event. put another way: every contact
leaves a trace. put it another way: haunting as repetitive strain injury.
13) robin james, *resilience & melancholy: pop music, feminism, neoliberalism,* (john hunt
publishing, 2015). really? nice work if you can get it.
14) as in the 13th century *tromdámh guaire.* see, bards are trouble, always have been.

the idiot dead / utterly beyond satire[15] // f-uh / house / ous
/ say / abounding in / a burdensome grace / at pains to take
/ up space / your beauty / swims / the width of my
working-out / and theory fails / to function / your death
/ is flesh made maverick / *a bomb is everything a building
was / devilish dust*[16] / a poem / is everything a body was /
horrible angel / i tighten the bolt / in your neck[17] / with a
safe pair of hands // in a meeting / fifteen minutes / talk
about / *catholic ghettos*[18] / you are / so angry / you shake /
rain prickles the skin / of a dark pond / and a partial mania
/ we're stuck / with each other / monotonous bodies in
space / conform / to the limp math holding /the universe
together / strong force / weak / force / the symbols / are
snug in / their brackets / spooning / like honeymooners /

15) because *guaire* was a braggart whose boast was he'd never been satirised. he invited the
poets in with all due hospitality and they outstayed their welcome by feeding off of him like a
load of locusts. he got what he deserved, but you take my point? yous are like boggarts, a kind
of poltergeist, once welcomed in impossible to extract. you know this about yourself, right?
16) from eyal weizman, *forensis: the architecture of public truth,* (sternberg press, 2014). the
way in which absence is registered. war isn't told through happenings but gaps. for instance:
this dust was a building. for instance: what happened to liam?
17) because like frankenstein's monster i am some kind of revenant? the poem as unhallowed
art, etc? it's camp too, in a way. it isn't frightening anymore, it's too ubiquitous. until you really
think about it. and ulster's steeped in those images, lumbering cartoon bogey men. grotesque.
in the proper sense.
18) they keep on saying this. as if *ghettos* are chosen, elective and sinister. ghettos are done
to people. there's a point you just stare at the dirty brown water and you're too exhausted for
pride.

Hyena! **Jackal!** Dog!

this is called / economics // hire purchase[19] / right to buy[20] / and other / thatcherite wheezes / like seany's head / with brains *blown out* / where the wound is a slogan / where a dead baby / becomes a slogan / a catch all chant / you can fit / in your mouth / your mother / *never got over it / the shit she seen* / you said / was everything / we passed a hat for // *executor* / or / *executioner* / these job descriptions come / with hoods / accidental archivist /misguided good intentions / distortion and omission / the body as magnetic tape / you're everything my instinct clings to / what's left / presumptuous zero / bridges alert with lights / *you're from london, yes?* / no / watermark / we mark / the water / enter here / inter / here / her / i mean / tear here / cut / i parse my sickle traits / my phobic blood / shame fits / like the skin of an apple / squeaky tight / you float / in the centre of my headache / lily / of the valley[21] / we are / *christians of the best edition / all picked and culled*[22] / inscrutable mood /

19) instalment plan. through which we pay, for ford cortinas with leaky radiators, fridge freezers, colour tvs. or did. payday loans are much better, though, aren't they? i wasn't using my fucking kneecaps for anything.
20) because you'd want to, wouldn't you? put up a picket fence, all pampas grass and plastic windmills. make you proud.
21) in a jar. on your windowsill. true believer. your faith frightens me. the pull of any inherited thing.
22) françois rabelais. Obviously.

in classrooms / my *temporary body* / my *pattern of events*[23] /
here's a document for you / canonical honey //

23) commissions are for shit. truth is not uncovered but constructed. sweet baby, you of all
people should know that.

Hyena! **Jackal!** Dog!

In the Emerald City

my friend is face-down, consulting her
hangover like a map. or else she is dead.
in a city like this is the pleasing secret
picked clean, the microclimate quick to
tears. *tell me who you are.* i'm all
the darkness draining from an eye. go
on, do the dead in different voices. do
the *our father* and the *gratia plena.* do
daddy issues. do the *girl crush.* do
the *predatory lesbian.* i'm a glacier
calving in a warm tumbler full of bells.
in the emerald city, an insect phrase,
closed against colour. *how do you like
me now?* would roundly slut my ethic
skin. the carnal hairpin *noir* of witches.

by which i mean – not that you asked –
they like you better dead, pressed to
their own piqued kink, gassed or slit
or *bombed out* of their ovaries on
pills, a row of gracious cabbages. eskar
of an old wound, how they hate. dames,
they want you good and doomed, and all
your limpid oeuvries debauched in
scalloped cotton. three women
in a room is a coven by default.
three poets in a room is fucking
riot. oh, those amatory zealots,
severed heads in a bowling bag.
listen, to cut it in the emerald city,
you've got to be tough, feet planted
firmly apart and screaming: *come at*
me, bro! with a fidgety vigour, all
omnicompetent female badass. my friend
says we shall never make it. pain is
a convex blues strained through lyric's
syrupy extremes – edel, idyll, idol: weiss,
weiss, weiss! – my contrarian austerity
will never be enough. failure of medicine
and *strict machine.* i have come to
fragrance under ailment, a way of being
wrong at which the dog sniffs, the nose,

irked in its turn with dying. i am old,
and my face is a sprawling proposal.
what are the symptoms? a circular rash
like the bite of a wolf. fever's dull urging.
exhaustion, turning, is a wire dreidel.
the enigma of ordeal, my gravel kingdoms
regained. but oh, we are so remorselessly
alive. season of doleful cirrus, spindrift,
loosestrife's louche anathema. in the emerald
city they pull us up as weeds. herbicide
and baling wire. haul me over the burning
coals of grim contention. by the roots
of my hair, by the picking of my thumbs,
by the screaming of my leukocytes. anaemia's
fatigue. the diminished marrow sings.
my friend, the neon crown she tilts to
rakish emblem. we were found wanton
at the animal fair. all the great old men
were there: sleekly dulapped in a staring
match with a stubbs cow. stuffed
and mounted. or antic, ripping wipers
off a ford cortina, gripping bent aerials
with their ugly prehensile iambs. listen,
the emerald city is full of zoos. vindictive
with sin. abattoirs: the punch-drunk
patiency of bovine, pedestrians, walking

pensions, students. in the emerald city
they ask to see your identity papers. *tell
us who you are.* we too have turned
to compost on the pillow, turned the pillow
into compost, run through your dreams
like a raptor on stilts, like a swan in
drag, a diseased mouth enriched on
its own emetic enormity, gorged
against grace. we know what they say
about us, a kind of do not resuscitate
daymare. 'cause they want you to be
a luminous dummy, all hankering
exploits and an intermittent signal. oh,
emerald city, fuck you. girl with
promiscuous ditches for eyes, fraggle
with nettles, her lines will harden
into symmetry. some cloistered furtive
screw, and the hopeless promptings
of a serious man grown thin in holding
back a laugh, fat in holding in a yawn.
when our lips move he slumps, tiredly
farting. *women, there is a difference
between elegance and grace, and you,
surpassingly slag. and you, spilling over
with the soft grey fervour of a stranger.
let me design you a while, until you are*

a ribboned cipher in your own stale works.
my friend and i, we will burn the emerald
city to the ground. yes, we fed communion
wafers to the cows. we drank their simmering
milk from the teat. shrews now, wasps, or
peevishly feline. no. a pit bull bitch. your
ripped throat a fillet of sweet fondness.
your fingers yet, your prizes too. oh enviable
world we have fucked to sufferance. everything
everything, wild green spoils.

Hyena! **Jackal!** Dog!

Jagged little pilot

take twice daily with food / shots fired / through the window
of a white wedding / swallow your intolerance / caught / in
the convex mirror / of your own desire / extending a tac-
tical hand / across /a trough / a swill / of lilies / you'll be
scraping his entrails / up / with a spade / in the valley / the
cows cling to their meat / derrida said / his future doom /
has always stalked / your friendship[1] / mourn / to mourn /
to mourne[2] / nothing up my slieve[3] / st john's[4] acetic head
/ smiling / like a skinned grape[5] / today was / academics

1) "[this is] the mourning that is prepared and that we expect from the very beginning...."
jacques derrida, (p. 146) *the work of mourning,* university of chicago press, 2001.
2) the mourne mountains, a granite mountain range in county down in the province of ulster.
immortalised by percy french in 1886 with what became the folk-band staple "the mountains
of mourne".
3) slieve donard, the highest peak in the same range of mountains.
4) both st john's point, county down, from which the mournes are visible. also st john, son of
cairlánd, for whom the area is named. the point is a possible location of a tenth century shrine
church dedicated to a saint whose legend has all but disappeared from history.
5) from the practice of preserving the bones of saints, including skulls, as holy relics.

/ pickled in their disciplines / you were / encircled by ring roads[6] / a swan was a silent dress[7] / you were a swan / you consented to feathers / autumn in norglen[8] / the leaves / are falling like fingernails / *dear mrs lock / we cannot disclose / i return*[9] / an unqualified eye to the text / you will meet him here / forever and nowhere / else / *dear mrs lock* / you are not lovely / you are leaking[10] / myopic / astonished / deface the parade from the photos / sporting your blood in a psych ward again / the fire has dined / on those you love / you might have loved / who might have loved / a girl like a pillow fight / falling piano / a face you can heave at the sea / not even the sea could / *dear mrs lock*/ cringing and lurking / by turns to the mouth / of a long barrow[11] / bored in the earth // *take twice daily with food* / double take / the eye / snaps back on itself / in a freakish light / you need / some

6) turf lodge in west belfast, being literally encircled by ring roads, making the area "unfortunately popular" with joy riders.

7) from an anglo-saxon riddle in the book of exeter: "silent is my garment /when i tread the earth / or dwell in the towns / or stir the waters..."

8) norglen, west belfast.

9) from the official response to a request for release of material held on self and family members by the london met. also other institutional interventions.

10) "all god's children are not beautiful. most of god's children are, in fact, barely presentable. the most common error made in matters of appearance is the belief that one should disdain the superficial and let the true beauty of one's soul shine through. if there are places on your body where this is a possibility, you are not attractive — you are leaking." fran lebowitz, (p.6) *metropolitan life*, e.p. Dutton, 1978.

11) newgrange, a neolithic monument located near the river boyne five miles from drogheda.

Hyena! **Jackal!** Dog!

perspective / they said / a face you can leave / by the edge of
the sea / you can fold with your clothes / at the edge of the
sea / not even the sea / could claim a face / like yours / the
unguessable dark inside a marble / the sleeve has emptied
itself / of birds / a watch is a wound we wear on the wrist
/ keeping / the creeping ten carat time / of all unwanted
things / you were not / what god intended / *dear mrs lock*
/ what they cannot disclose / is a voice that sings / hey /
neither you are you / nor home is home[12] / nor home is home
nor home / nor / glen / acute impossible melancholy / suck-
ing a hardboiled hash tag / heard a girl / say / *rape baby*[13] /
you need / some *perspective* / hamill[14] / is to hold / hostage
to a name / to / a mutilated namesake / scarred / stretched
/ like a skin of a drum / and a man / with knives for teeth
/ romancing his advantage / in a hospital corridor / you
must allow yourself to be / *occupied* / by other voices / they
crowd your mouth like curses / crowd your mouth / red
velvet / fully / upholstered / in profanity / cunt like cinema
bucket seat / *rape baby* / *dear mrs lock* / *we cannot disclose*

12) from the poem fragment by abu tammam, 788 – 845, a damascan poet and muslim
convert, best known for compiling the ḥamāsah, considered the first and still one of the finest
compilations of arabic poetry.
13) from the article *the legitimate children of rape,* andrew solomon, the new yorker, august 29
2012, and the internet comments surrounding the publication of this article.
14) from the irish ó haghmaill, who claim descent from 6th centurary king niall noígíallac, or
niall of the nine hostages, whose historicity is dubious at best.

/ *distance*/ is the lipstick / between your bottom lip / and its most / dangerous profession // *take twice daily with food*/ snow white / in a crown of expendable swallows / this is the line in the sand / between mourning / and melancholy[15] this / is a border crossing / you / are smuggling thorough-breds[16] / dead men insisting like whitman / i am the man / i suffered / i was there[17] / hunger will make mystics of us all[18] / in the end / pervert the polarity[19] / travel back in time / quicklime and bitumen / byzantine fire[20] / panic / insinu-ates / ensues / consumes / a spider in the corner / artific-ing silk / from silence / from names that take the shape of cravings / mícheál / martyn / daddus / home / today was academics / shrink wrapped in their disciplines / practice /

---

15) "in mourning it is the world which has become poor and empty; in melancholia it is the ego itself." (p. 246) sigmund freud, *mourning and melancholia*, penguin classics, uk edition, 2005.

16) from the practice of smuggling horses across the irish border into the republic.

17) "how the lank loose-gowned women looked when boated from the side of their prepared graves, / how the silent old-faced infants, and the lifted sick, and the sharp-lipped unshaved men;/ all this i swallow, it tastes good, i like it well, it becomes mine, / i am the man, i suffered, i was there." (p.25) walt whitman, *heroes* penguin classics, 1961.

18) from the ascetic practice of self-torture by starvation as promoted by christian mystic sects as early as the 2nd century. also, the political protests of irish republican hunger strikers. also, the self-starvation of anorexic girls. the contention that context makes meaning from pathological, self-injurious behaviour. that culture makes this differentiation in a way this poem does not.

19) a variation on "reverse the polarity", a popular sci-fi cure all on tv series doctor who during the 70s.

20) an incendiary weapon developed and popularised during the byzantine empire but whose exact composition is lost to history, forms of so called "greek fire" were still in use during the time of the irish civil war, defined as (mainly clay) projectiles, filled with explosive or flammable compounds, most likely various ratios of bitumen or quicklime.

Hyena! **Jackal!** Dog!

the erudition of derangement / cultivate / the sugar coated
pill / that rides you like a nightmare / like the nightmare /
that you are / jagged little pilot / your captain and your par-
asite / teach you how to hold your hand / as steady as metal
wing / a steel edge / the dead / flow over / luckless currents
/ the suffering air.

Hyena! **Jackal!** Dog!

To disappear into

the mushroom-grower's gloom
of an unmade bed; the city, a stale
disgorging sky behind me. or
to step into the forest, a reticent
light filtered through cypress
and pine. for the longest time,
my compass, caressed into spin;
precautions and disguises
to mitigate against myself. there
has always been a forest,
its canopies and tangles; pairs
of jacks and plugs. complete
the circuit, connect the call.
there has always been a pressure,
building like a dialtone. indifferent

dissolve of heat or stars. i could
walk. i walk. the wind has
its own scripture: vague
persuasions, exasperated
soughing. sounds like any
prowling friend, mouth
rippled into aimless kinship:
try to think positive! take up
yoga and protein shakes! take
up thy bed! lips chapped to
bald cheek on mantras of self-
care. i cringe from such
mindfulness, like a dog
cringes from fireworks.
the forest buttons its mufti
against the wind, against
the friends, those pouncers-
out of doorways, their grease-
proof pieties, ponderous
professions over flakes
of golden pastry. they are not
the worst. there are rip-off
merchants, remission's
bitches, silly boys who fete
you for the sake of it, would slake
their morbid notions in you.

Hyena! **Jackal!** Dog!

there are doctors.

the forest does not care.
the forest is a keyhole. the forest
is a clenched jaw. is anything
tight against the world. the forest
has hollow bones, ice caves hostile
to hibernation. it does not soil itself
with tigers; is a cold kiln casting
animals in glass, and me among.
speaks with a salt asperity,
breath of the true sea, and all
of its trees read zero. a fever
below. i like a still cold stinging
me: suffused, incised. my frigid
insteps tend to glass, my skin
a shining turquoise bowl.
snow, glowing like luminol.
a towering ash, tall keratin
tusk, hoarfrost's softly vascular
skin, velvet's ripped *excelsior.*
to step into the forest is to change.
be a shed antler lain upon needles,
to glow. there was always
a forest. i would walk toward
but never reach, postponed

among power lines; recompense
and pethidine, not wanting
to hurt. and the lilting consideration
of lovers. and the orthodox solemnity
of a white bird passing; a whitsun
seagull sprung eternal. there was
always hope. until there wasn't.
the forest isn't *full* of ghosts, but
maybe one or two, whose unleavened
eyelids droop, who stir turnips into
the frozen earth, expecting them to grow.
and i don't mind that. there to abide
in the shipwreck of my life's esteems,
soprano in a violent choir and for
all time. no more of ration's reign.
no more carbolic blocks of thought,
tepidly soaping the brain.
the city lacquers its enchantments.
the mad in their niches, perpetual
staggering transit, the grudging
gruntwork of consent. in the city,
the guillotines are preening. i want
that vertical march to the light.
to be free. to disappear, from
stigma and sophistry, sad paranoia;
from the one-up men, their arsenal

of idle hands. and most from desire,
drilling into a tooth; the swivelling
impulse, spectacle and frenzy.
in time lapse and aggro, sleep.
in a maze of my own waking, null
and veering, doing the crazy again.
the tricksy graphics of a feedback
form. reproof, reproach, a desperate
under-signing. i want the forest.
maligned in silence, sleep. i want
to sleep. see me jink and flicker
from the path. my truest form
is weightless, the straying
of a single leaf.

Hyena! **Jackal!** Dog!

Délires

all along, a child, rawly lingering.
concrete crossed to climax: a cold
dawn wrought with fault. have held
this for a felony's stretch. concussed
on endless buses to a circular theme.
gape, decay. the traffic of it. thin rain
threading the failed semis together.
typical and stilted, walk our bland
arousal to devouring. indelible now,
through snow to stint a smoker's
cough in cancer wards and worse,
a carceral pub. drink deprivation's
sediment, and spit. have held this
storied stark-unworthy, crawled
in crowds. men, in the welders'
masks of anonymous mourning.
a skin to score their graphics

of detachment. patient pugilists,
knuckles plump as pillows. all
along. a song to learn the limits
of malaise. someone says: starve
an axe, feed a forest. near-sighted
smear of meaning on a weeping
window. mortal and comic, face
the out-of-focus firmament. grin.
sword-swallower's smile, you had.
formed queues, convened relief
committees out of affluence.
architects are starry-eyed to
frame your flagging nerve in
wet cement. acutely cradled,
wiring the retardant dark for
fire. now literate with demolition.
how sinister and reverent, the touch
that builds a new bohemian amenity.
raised, from the silence of your
seizures. everybody singing:
attrition, contrition, mass-
market ambition. flood the street
to blight our nursery blood. our
ghetto is a legend writ large in
a urinal now. infestations, alchemies.
rehearsing the hurt space, over

and over. oh, love, gone sauntering
and mortified to quiet capitulation.
your names, abruptly underlined
in all my notebooks of return.
developer, who folds his crisp
affection like a cheque. carotid
glut, the blood is barely breathing
through its clots and smuts, and all
the leather sticklers out here taking
the air. have held this. misaffection,
malocclusion. teeth that will not
meet. between cusp and groove,
the spoon, the strap. grasp this focal
flailing one last time with feeling,
leaning into loneliness. have held
this, in the meningital stare of sell-
outs, default of doubtful tenderness.
and now, and now, the branded
anomie. memory, confined, refuted,
sold. sun struggles through
its watery ascensions still. and men
are tall with money, turned toward
the vivid doom of lochs and squats
and prodigies. the dead with their
stocks of sunken gold. conspiracy
of scythes, reap the gilded ribs

of dancehalls, erect a stout saint
before the door in yellow hi-vis.
have held this, have seen you drink
this rippling brilliance to spree.
slouched and sopping. towns
assume their ruin; the eye intent on better
jewelling makes its myths. in celibate times
have paced our burning missteps out. errant
and engulfed. where holding frays, is forged.
accelerant, deceit. the spaces in between.
teetering bleakness. its depots
and its despots too. city is the circle.
grey eyes, green eyes, idling
carnivores. all along, were children.
the ugly mechanical cosseting. chewed
cheek hanging in shreds. snail trails,
caterpillar sophistries. the tracks we left,
are left of us.

Dog!

Hyena! Jackal! **Dog!**

'Heritage'

here, your most absolute eye
is green. no, brown. no, blue.
i do not recall. all the fertile
trespass of a rural aching. i
should take the pheasant track
to slow astonishment and say
this is an unfolding. or, i
unfold. i do; my dreams are
fire unfolded to incendiary
certainty. i conflegarate my
enemies; first of all is you.
liber ignium, book of fires,
book on fire, a burning
book. nitrate's bitter tithes.
there is such violence in me,
the fire lance, the wire flail.

and yours, the the sun wheel
always. i will drain
the spitting fortune crouched
in cups, and swilling every
miracle to soot. black tea
will bite the taunting from
your tongue. silence.
sniffing your own sulphur.
a spade's graft is
the measure of my time.
and blood, my true
blood. i have pictured
your death a thousand
ways, a thousand-
thousand prim occasions
never sorry. but,
for all my swinging
pendulums and burning
windmills, you
have grown old. you
will expire in the flat sloth
of a hospital, breathing
the dust of your own
soaped entropy; used skin
falling in dry drifts like snow.
a bee stings once. a wasp

is a repeat offender. acid
hymns to his own recidivist
cruelty, knows no season.
it's coming back. you
are coming back, and there
will not be hoods enough for
hanging, shirt-fronts wide
enough to sew our shame,
our liquid labours
flowing back into the pure
brown mouth ripped wide.
between baxt and ladž
the lathe, the lyre, the guillotine,
the lead perfection of a fugue.
here, your most absolute eye
is a death-glyph, a word from
which the lips recoil, writhing
in salt, in candle fat, in the socket
of a skull: maggot in a bruise.
there was a white face,
disfigured by symmetry.
the thicket, the abyss, how
all our footsteps tend in transit.
yes, there was a bottle, a smoke-
wreck sunk inside. there was a
can of poisoned peaches. there was

a line of naked women walking at
the point of something sharp.
here, it could happen here. i stare
at you. you don't even blink.

Internal medicine

my dog will come back as an arsonist. look at him,
he's pissing on the places he will later want to burn.
i might not come back at all. if i do, don't name me
after a saint, mother. invite the wind into your mouth,
name me after a hurricane. i wish i'd thrown my
former lovers from the bridge, instead of just their
trinkets. pain inside, drink a glass of sympathetic
vinegar. pain inside, i am wolf with it. in the night
a caesarian of dancing piglet stones somehow. how
pain becomes the knots my words refuse. a pain
that won't be fumbled to dissolving in the canny clinic
of the bed, the bath, the pumpkin-cutter's kitchen
drecked with pulp. mother, they stole my photo for
a government campaign. they dressed me in another
name, filched from a politically correct math
problem. mother, i am like lenigrad. no, stalingrad.

no, petrograd. no, mother i am fatimagrad. all my
citizens beavering for minimum in cyber. i walk up
the stairs, it does that auto-redial thing, the pain.
i open my face like a guidebook, a fold-out map to
torment's ease. i swallow all the buttons from a long
white coat. now the doctor will be naked and the tap
water tastes of rust. let's go round the block again
dog, round streets we only ever learnt by scent. let's
walk. walking helps, although the windows shit
their scenery: women with functioning loins
in boden dresses, picking the burs out of spaniel
ears, tucking the mixed recycling in for the night.
glass jars in this one, a row of obedient embryos,
and a couple of elderly vampires, discussing
the bouquet of blood. let's burn it down, dog. cross
the road. i'm smiling like a stallion, joyfully skinned.
my scathed companion, let's go slow. i swear dog,
at the mess inside of me the knives turn timid. you
are the same. imagine putting a cigarette out in
a handshake. imagine all the coins in a money box
melting together. imagine crunching
a glass eye like an ice-cube. it's all
those things and less. i can't explain. what if
this curdling forensic dark were my true voice?
mother, open me up. pull out the sugar shrimps,
the molotovs, the miles of strawberry bootlace.

Hyena! Jackal! **Dog!**

Poem in which i became a bear

and fled to the sawtoothed haunts
of the forest, distended and gestating.
the bear had been swelling inside
of me – a cervical cyst with a thicket
of hair – since ninety-eight. *unkindly*
form, unkempt and eager-eyed. all
her stares were sidelong. bear would
be born, a stiff aura of fur, radiating
outwards like a halo from my cunt.
sundered, surrendered, not knowing
how to say. so *bear.* you could drown
in bear, all your precious memories
accessible to fire. bear would be
worn on the outside. not your soft
bear: stuffed animal eyes turned
to the wall. no, not a *stuffed* bear,

but a girl *stuffed* with being bear.
this crypt of thistles. hair-quake,
hair-waltz, a carny's horny bearded
bride. a bear is a threshold. a bear
is a fur terminus. carnivoran
frontier, self-lubricating howl.
in the forest i licked my shame
to shape. there were tremors,
there was vomit. until i became
upholstered in bear, until i became
a sprinting crouch, bellowing my
bleak disclaimers to the hills:
come at me! i dare you! my mouth
grew long, innovating bayonets;
i gathered mass. pick the crust
off a girl, there's a bear beneath.
he thinks he did this. they think
i think he did this. they think
i am sorry. a bear is a stain becomes
part of the design. i have eaten men
alive, corrupted and replete,
i have hugged my own consoling
bulk all night long. between
maiden and *mother*, a bear. her
shape stirred into the circumpolar
sky like nuts in fucking yoghurt.

not a skybear, i. no azimuth. no
altitude. no *catalogue of stars.*
i choose the damp earth under
me, close enough to him to
take off his head.

Hyena! Jackal! **Dog!**

Iphigenia

stapled eyelids, steepled fingers, *sleep*.
my telescope has sleuthed the swarming
stars for signs. by *telescope* i mean my
eye. my eye is a torchbearer, rearing
its manifold fires. my fires, leaping in
relays. there's a light inside of men, both
permanent and obsolete. this moon has
bitter marvels; banalities and guises,
throes. some monster stalks my
ornamental histories, sluggish scent
of vervain, silver cimaruta, all my
apotropaic charms. staunch and bane.
my ruing herbs. and i would sleep,
succumb to its eddying medicine. but
sleep is a false friend, and plenty enough
of that when i'm – stare into the riddling

abyss of self-absorption; the mirror
turns my calculations jagged, my saffron
robes to rope. i come at myself
obliquely in a semi-circular motion;
my eyebags are crowded with cotton
balls. a girl is a kind of professional
orchid. my veil becomes oblivion;
i practice myself through a fine
tulle mesh. oh girling fate, textbook
of transparencies. *maiden*
is a codliver word mutating
in a liturgical spoon. i know what's
coming. father on the stairs, creaking
to correct my gravity. he's prepared
the pyre, a parafin digression
among the heaped briquettes.
a *big man* now, all his principals
distilled to oath inside a smokey
glass. a bad day concentrate
in a chipped tooth, in a nicked
chin, in tiny tissue paper squares.
his uniform, buttoned to comeuppance,
and up he comes. something shiny
and primitive is polishing itself along
the edge of my presentiment. his eyes
are running like undercooked egg. he

has muck on his boots; he bears the green
dirt like a perfume, has kicked
the malfunctioning flora into heaps.
there's a knot tied in his tight, white
binding. my spine is a ribbon for
stringing beads. here is the night's
girdling hand. my thighs move into
alignment. he says my name. my name
becomes a blush becomes a tunnle
to redundancy.

Hyena! Jackal! **Dog!**

My life as a popular frieze

i had my cults and carvings,
xoanon and effigies, small
wonders worked in wood.
i laid the path. i made
the mark. from ipecac,
a rhizome dried, i drew
the dark. set spinning
sun and moon. this world
was never yours, you
softboiled boys. but now
my sheeted icons stare
from cat-piss peeling corners.
and the room is bare. listen:
egged on and three-sheets
on shore leave, peleus liked
a sickle place in me;

my filaments and lamellae.
my fertile surface. fruiting
body firm. these gills, these
scales, more lachrymose
mouths. *cry all you want,*
decanting the day's quota
of honeyed doom into
the shape of me. i had my
acolytes, my aspects, all
my subtle ways of raving.
his damask, anaglypta,
chintz, a theory of hysteria.
wandering womb, my
chambered brain was
wayward. honeycomb's
compressive strength,
my suspect structures
riddled from within. i
was a snake, was a lion
in a fire, and a strong wind
wheeling his ship
toward the rocks.
his was an abductor's
grip. proficient finger,
crooked to fishook pun.
caught, *landed,* gaping.

Hyena! Jackal! **Dog!**

would strip entreaty
out of air. had i breath.
the taste of his flesh
burns brackish. i
am a razor shell, pried
apart. i had my rites
and prophesies: in
nine months time
they'll hang me at
the end of the jetty
like a shark, slit
my belly and see
what falls out –
a licence plate
a glass amphora
a mostly mortal child.

Hyena! Jackal! **Dog!**

Saverland v Newton, 1837

'When a man kisses a woman against her will, she is fully enti-
tled to bite his nose off, if she so pleases.'

and what if i should? and fall to biting, regular.
impulse, caprice, infatuation's fangs. what if i
should – *fantastic affection* – spread infection's
folly? intuitive contagion. you know what
women are. fury rising up, all sudden mouth,
excited fancy's flood. i read about those german
nuns, feral with suppression. minky girls in
a poacher's sack. anywhere a tooth draws blood,
i might – bite back, backbite, develop a taste
for human flesh: flytrap, pitcher, pout and flay.
sundew's suffocating glue. secrete, ensnare,
my sticky lips. cobra lily's acid bath. be
butterwort or byblis. slick rosette. asphyxia's
fly-paper fronds. orchids sleek and crude
with cannibal enzyme. *aldrovanda,* aquaria's
vampire queen. i read about those plants.

i read the lurid yellow books to sweat. i dreamt
myself in therian and harpy. a lycan's kiss
in steaming fur. what if i should, if dreams
come true? your shattered reefs, your domes
and scrolls quite sacked, my dear. cartilage,
your septal carthage trashed. what if? how
it might be, *your* integrity torn like a forger's
brand, your freak-face fit for pity's paper bag,
foreboding meat measured for its mask. touch
me again, kindle these carnivore tumults in me.
i will sharpen my instruments a while. come
closer, love, i'm sizing up the horn by which
i'll fasten hold.

'Merry Tuft'

i.m Mary Toft

an' not so *merry.* i was working the fields, some
spiculate malignancy stirring inside. i was tired,
my head aching like bad schnapps, and hunger's
trumpets shaking everything to shit. i was *big
with child.* i was eve's sad *defixio*, picked into lead
with a nail. there was hot fat hissing at the skillet's
centre. an' pain began its time-conditioned spin.
baby, massa peccati, mass of sin. wanted rabbet
in tang an' tussle, in flinty meat, an' taut an' flying
form. i ran too fast. the *baby* failed, an' not my first,
an' not my last. my body is a morgue. so little to eat.
i dreamt of rabbet every night, tight inside the amber
girdle of his stare. my *rasselbock* my *jackalope.* no,
not a rabbet, but a hare! weaving through my warrens,
all the body's secret wynds. men. men of science, men
of god, you ask who *cooked it up*? his entrenched

step upon the stair, a husband's rights, the gothic snot
that falls from us, bundled like a boiling sheet. no one
cooked. our rawest scheme. credulous or cunning?
take your pick. idiots. i came not to intrigue but to
reproach. my monsters not *imposture*, but an
allegory. you see? you do not see. fanatic action
of a hand. your slick insertions, scrutinies. i said my
prayers to the hare of the field and spat in a pail
of rancid milk. up leapt my varmint offspring. she's
leaping still. to roam my rookeries at night. eostre
fleet in a leveret light.

Witch's mark

ripped up the carpet in the red room: a cache
of tangent circles. hexafoil, my gothic lily. in
every house a secret witch's mark. beseeching
scratch, the scare quotes round a perishable
name. i'd fill a dish with plump sultanas. rake
your draggle alphabets into the wooden boards.
to ward or to invite. how night sloughs off
the corset of its forms. hollow light, draining
from a horned moon, yellow and suspended.
there was nothing left to do. fear in all the claret
follies of its clutching came. my chaste fables
of protection would not serve: the cold ash
and the stout cord; a silver cross, the bronze
bullae, a single thaler sewn inside the mouth.
the last was fire, a word, a scab of wax, picked
soft. how bodies are bartered and bound. how

the dark is drawn in, tight as a purse. when it
did not work. at night i've said the spell of it:
morose, remorse, a rose i cull with care.
going forth by day the sun inscribes its curse,
the enigmatic cancers of my witch's skin. my
witch's marks, my suckle-luck grown big.
legions, weals, and welts. elitely eyed, motif
of wheels. my blemishes, my devil dials, this
detail: hag stone in my stomach. i will tear it
to atonement after every meal. palm crossed
with its own claw. this, my fate. i made a poor
witch. horsehair lore. my dollies rot their
widdershins. you slept above the hexafoil,
grew thin and pale as dirty straw. i am still
here. ambition's black canals, alive and yet –
terror, with the next deft shift of the sea, i'm
gone. the cauldron's brine resolve. the ram,
the goat, accused, accursed. maiden. crone.
the water's whorled worst. this drowned
face, my own.

Magic yet

my waking thoughts are woeful.
in washed-out porches, pumpkins
grin like bailiffs. streets of a circling
stillness walked to the arrogant
hastening of pain. and i want my
boxty bread, barmbrack charms.
nutcrack night. my soulcake-
scoffer's liturgy. they do not know,
their strictly-steepled churches
probe the upper air like dentists'
drills. the crack-head has his
baritone; his wire bride, her
tremolo. a wilderness of wheelie
bins. love and its fallible
rigmarole. yesterday's news,
a skeleton libretto. dear brecht, we

are beyond all singing now. men
who talk enchantment into
platitude. a dumb face, begging
a bruise. i want my corpse path,
darling, my phantom light, acetic
sting, ascetic stomach shrunk on
gruel and yellow: cider vinegar's
gilding. i want the apple bobbed
to drowning. the powdered glass,
the killer clown, the witch's aga
wide enough for scout troops. give
me red legs scattering silver
dollars, chocolate money. give me
that old time religion, there's power
in the blood. not this. inane
and fatal day, when government
men fall to their botching with
sawbone elbows out. oh larks,
oh jollies. i'll keep my small fire
here. tealight in a hollow gourd.
spectral heat. like hope.

RED BIDDY

red biddy

noun

a mixture of cheap wine and methylated spirits.

biddy

noun

of unknown origin; probably influenced by the
use of *biddy* denoting an Irish maidservant,
from *Biddy*, pet form of the given name *Bridget* .

'All you young people now take my advice
Before crossing the ocean you'd better think
twice'– Jimmy MacCartey

.1

ever hear the one about the man with two shadows?

one was a matador's cape, the other a thin girl cut from the queasy cloth of her own bad self. this is a monday, mind. fire weaving hawkweed into hacking cough. he slipped his plimsolls running. leapt the fence. spread his hand to find his cocksure fortune full of thorns. took his torn palm into town, tarried his swaggering luck through lanes. bantam boy, bantering, jaw-jacked scally in the jackdaw dawn. his aggie ma, hauling his name across coals all the days of her life, till it rose on the roof of her mouth like a blister. scar of his slingshot pedigree. he'd never come back, each delinquent sinew stretched its short electric measure. said his going *ripped the lining* from her eyes. if sons were *sovvies*, silvered in the silk-purse of her seeing. said she wore his beaming counterfeit smooth across one side. and oh, he was the ether's genii then, dreamt his chequered pleasures, walked each night towards the guillotine of sleep with baby steps. he was *away*, trailing his lustrous brawn through forecourts, car parks, foreclosed farms. following the bitter ribbon of the road to the north, to the west, to the ford-mouth of the hostings, to the old men buckled by husbandry, gingham girls in the grip

Hyena! Jackal! **Dog!**

of small town non-event. and oh, that canny lad, that dia-
mond bruiser, that one time baron of ballinasloe –

and this was the man with two shadows? tell me.

i was coming to that. always i was coming. how he slept
under hedges. his shadow was his pillow and his bindle and
he carried the whole world knotted up in one wet corner of
it. how he was spring's pilgrim, hobnail apostle of the copse
and culvert, anything cooked in a smoky hole. and it was
thin going, till the whole dark sea laid out before him like a
lead apron. and he paid his passage in *coarse words for com-
mon objects,* and his passage was long, and he slept standing
up like a horse. how sometimes you're not even moving,
how a hard road travels the length of a man, his romanestan
swelling and stretching inside. and he slept on the docks in
his shadow, bound in its red-green wastrel cloak. and blue.
when a man's hand is his flag, and you can read his shadow
like the grimoir of his poxy fate, and his mother's voice in
an auger shell, on and on, remorseless and rokkering. god.
in liverpool they tell him his gold tooth's got by alchemy,
and they try his gilded tongue for passing twice through a
wishing ring, and they sharpen their telepathy on the edge
of a desk, and cut down the tree on which his mother carved

his birth, and his mother's voice ran silent then, as a stream runs mud.

is all this true?

yes. and his first shadow was a sling, and he carried his arms and his hunger in it. and his own mother wouldn't know him from a scarecrow. and they called him *scrub tinker*, not even fit for sorting scrap. and he chewed all night on his daddy's blackberry blood, mulled her pale face too, poor cow, who bore her grief like a basket of knives and could not love him. he could not sit still. he would not be work of many hands. chased from verges, grim billets of wasteland. wanted away and he ran. but that tongue, lord, inching through the soily hours of darkness like a worm, has its own earth-cravings, must speak brick-dust dirt to loam, find a way to sing.

and of the other shadow?

saw *her* by the union chapel, hawley road, driving spears of heather through the plush lapels of enemy gents like she wanted them staked and dead. they were frisking her lingo for a telltale cluck when she spat in their faces: *talk to me about* resilience, *i'll grind your bones to make my bread.* pikey. worse. poshrat, answers to the suck of air between a plumber's teeth. and has no name. cuts her hair to a cold hearth breathing soot, and doesn't care. she has no tongue, she does not eat. nurses pry her teeth apart. all they find inside is another man's fist.

this shadow is dangerous.

yes. but how like himself. and takes his hand. flailing his workshy meat in a warehouse. body, a deviant dance against gravity. hard life. lucks into sudden colour when she is near. a gallon jug of thunderbird, a tin of tea. an ambulance racing somebody to somewhere in the painterly night. mad alan with his rat tattoo, gone off his trolley in a squat. the waify and immaterial few, whose high a rome where all these mainline mazes lead. these lesser roads. these vandals and these goths. london is a cloned ghost mouthing her sweet nothings in every window. is a window for every ghost. the squat, that squat, that garrison of discontent. the rec ground gone to nettles, mad behind paddington, sweating out its lairy yellow threat, its green seam split, its ambush of weeds. affrighted edge, the paring blade of *any*where.

london tests her raging mettle, his. lies with his back pushed into the earth, holding the whole world up by its ripped mattress. becomes a bootleg christ, sprawled and gormless against the plank he'll walk to crucifixion. oh, *she* says there's beauty in a daggered light like strangulation. folds him, strokes the clammy threads of his disorder smooth. bathes him in another name. not the moniker that swaddled him, but something rushy, wet. fixes his blood to hers with a razor's partial grace. her fingers falter holes in his lobes with a pin till he's pricked all over like a grubby bud of lace.

but how did they become tied?

i was coming to that. always i was coming. all her life, she said, she was smeared across the threshold of some man, worn in his buttonhole, drowned in his poacher's pocket. and she ran too. made herself anew from a ragbag of silky fixings. scraped herself from barrel bottoms, sucked the pennies out of fountains clean. read borrow. said *he's well named* and vexed his mildew-muddled ghost in stoppered bottles. read the world with gleaning eye, said *oh, i rue the day i dipped my biddy tongue in your foul cant.* england, where the torchlight traipses over her. where her pavee ariettas are the meat the organ grinds to tuneful mince. and

spoilt. she wanted the world. not to treasure, but to smash.
to master its daggers and turn them back on the hands that
held them, to drag their bleeding précis' through her patois'
gutter gorse, each faltering declension a barb in their moral
hide. he was too hurt. wanted the voodoo of spoons, the
sweet numb sleep, and a lasting drink of red. his vision driz-
zled into constellation. they have *no word for stars*, borrow
said. oh, but please, a fulsome argot of moons. she tied him
with her own cut hair. with shrove candles, baked apples,
their subtle fragrance sealed in heat, her own wrists swim-
ming in beeswax and blood, the golden sear on greyish meat,
the burning of bundles of sage. flimsy bonds. shapeless kite,
mithered by wind. barely snagged at her ravelled edge.

so they became torn?

in secret he'd fed his first shadow. it grew so big, shaking its
rusty antlers. wran jag mask, dancer at the wake. shadow
number one now a furbearing fluke of pain with his moth-
er's face. in his dreams the camp and the last of the fire,
eating through sleep's thin celluloid strips. and london's
vicious bridges, bearing his weary guilt on their backs.
coward, they called him, *cunning.* work was long when work
was to be had. and morning's fearsome cold enough to drive

the tattoos from his skin. he had no words, but those words going forth by day on the book of himself. how rocks tear the underbellies of boats, a thought of home would surprise him. where *home* is not a shore but a tongue that beg to wag. ganger, gavver, gaffer, they flattened him to *paddy,* poor *paddy*, a word with a chaser of bile brought forth from your own loathe gut. the north and its blethering fevers. a stubby finger stabbing his chest at closing time: *which side are you on?* until *home* is a chandelier sinking to the bottom of a wreck, is a dropped needle scoring a song through dusty shellac.

and so?

he ran. at first she clung to his back like a hump of his own dull flesh, but he slipped her when she was stringing her words into makeshift bandoliers some throbbing morning. how the last thing she said with a look like getting straight was *i don't know how to help you.* and he was going back. and she was eating the night into abstinence. her tongue could cut water. his formed a wick trimmed especial for poison tallow.

and so?

Hyena! Jackal! **Dog!**

he drank. he died.

and so?

you know. that look on her face, that body all lithe and pi-
ous, poised when you ask her where she's from to rip your
fucking throat out. you know full well. when she sits still and
throws a sundial's shape across paper. yes. did you hear the
one about the woman with two shadows?

'The older Biddy comes in three varieties: a sturdy, plain,
bossy woman with a broad face, pug nose, a topknot and
beefy forearms; a squat, simian-featured woman with a
grizzled muzzle and big feet who is given to helping herself
to household resources and to supporting Irish revolution-
aries; and most simian of all, Biddy Tyrannus, an enormous
menacing figure who threatens her employer...'
– Maureen Murphy, *Bridget and Biddy: Images of the Irish
Servant Girl in* Puck *Cartoons 1800-1890*

will it all come good?

unlikely.

when will it all come good?

hers is the *face of adversity*, an adverse face, hung from her head like a horse-brass. this *simian biddy* is the stove's hot doppelganger, matriarch of cloves. fire puts out its tongue to taste the brightness in *her* eye. kitchen-smith, sucker-up of pedant sauces: louth's gunpowder physic. lemongrass, then pepper, thyme. *this* to ward of fever – honey-stave – and *this* to do god's work. thumb the subtle gills of wild shiitake wide, and plumb the tureen's teeming depths. her stock contains bestiaries, vinegar multitudes. pick the demerara layer from sleep. she does not sleep. can balance her reflection in a brimming spoon. it is not wood she's burning, it's evidence, until her conscience runs as clear as her soup. ever bust a knuckle on a side of beef? hold up the hollowed-out slippers of fish, as if for some cinderella? studded dismal

bolts of dough with rosemary and sage? seen yourself in a
sheet of bonfire toffee and wished you could die, just die?
she is my dream, her and her calendar of tatties, my fate.
running round the covered market like a minotaur, terma-
gant for oranges. the butcher sells her porcine sawdust
prisoners, tied together at the waist. alone, she rubs the
patchy nap from a velvet word like *fealty,* soaking her feet in
a cracked plastic bowl.

won't she ever be free?

of what? famine wastes the figurines she's polished them
so hard, this *simian biddy.* purified the puffy faces of their
children with her own *fenian* spit. outside, the plum trees,
sagging with sweetness. a white rooster strutting like a pris-
on snitch between the condemned cell and the strawberry
beds. she's not immune to pain, it's what the *lower orders*
have in lieu of conscience. slipped disks and twinges. golem
of the sink. how one time she bit the head from a china shep-
herdess, she was so angry. they

pretend to be afraid of her. she's draining the grease from a
skillet like a sawbones bleeding a vein. they pretend to be
afraid. motes of brackish coffee circle the plug, and jeyes flu-

id worries her gloves of reddened flesh to temper. was your name ever a stone in your earshot? did you make a crown of poet's laurels from leaves of sweetheart cabbage? will *your* shape ever shuffle in the memory of mastiff dogs? are your caresses cudgels? do you save the stubs of candles? have you balled your gridlocked fists by your sides, while smart rejoinders breed in your apron pocket like skinny ferrets?

was it always so bad?

no. and that's the hell of it.

will it always be so bad?

scrubber. skivvy. scullion. drudge. let me answer your question with a question: have your lips been numb and blue from biting back a grudge? and have you ever had to separate the chicken from the pillow? are you a *simian biddy*? think carefully. could you hit your boss so hard you knock the dandruff from his roots, the spinach from between his teeth? could you pull a corset tight enough to crack a rib, to cut her damsel's waist in two? have you cleaned her house?

has she wrinkled her nose at your ripped raw skin? does
every third trip to the shops end in belligerent fisticuffs?
well, there you are. she is my dream. she has tied on her
face with a permanent scowl. she has fashioned her ringlets
from peel. in the heel of her boots she has hidden the hair
of her enemies. has seasoned their bisque with her men-
strual blood, has blown her nose on their scented towels.
don't laugh. weak sun. its lackpenny pendulum sets her in
motion. you could eat your dinner from this hardwood floor.
oh, her sleeves are wide enough for silverware. you'll not
catch her concussed by accusation. no *grovelling apology*.
and she has smuggled mahogany sideboards out under her
skirts, has skimmed the cream with her tongue, has smeared
her aching legs in your quack balms, has spiked your patent
specifics with ground up glass. in her tenement, potsherds
glint on a gimcrack mantle, and the fire curls the edges
of photographs. mildew, and at night the stains turn into
sons. her lovely boys. pictures pinned to cheap emblems of
wilderness: mummified sprays of heather. their dead eyes
gleam like toys.

biddy

noun

1. adult female chicken
2. young bird especially of domestic fowl
3. generic for an Irish maid
4. derogatory slang term for women
5. an elderly woman, regarded as annoying or interfering
6. slattern or prostitute

or

7. from the Celtic Brigit, meaning 'exalted'.

.3

this was her mountain, yes?

yes. where women are not killed so much as turned to birds.

and this was her name?

they made her a cipher for livestock. penance of cutthroat
sex. they said her name so that it sounded like a splayed
hand being soaped. they wrote papers about her, then slept,
twin hares jugged in a thick indifference. talked about the
time his cigarette made freckles. and *her* voice spilling its
own peculiar quarrel. a language *so* wide her teachers re-
moved their teeth with pliers.

when?

time of wiping his hands on a new growth of grass. time of
sudden *crack!*s sending shockwaves through a shadow and

it breaks apart as starlings. time of schemes for robbing the rainbow's end, when, up all night, she'd known them talk their teeth to air. time under a bridge. time of methylated alchemy. time of magpies, little hitmen, cocking a song at her temples. time of swallows, martens, every feted thrush. time of blackbirds, lilting their thrifty *waste not* warning to the formal dawn. time of music, pushing up through london's sodden bedrock, of bleeding in a moshpit, ecstatic as a sky on fire. time of women made from matchsticks, struck against the concrete walls of laundries. time of *green grows the lily-o,* and a rash on her hands from pulling up banes and worts by the root. time of skips and bins. time of fireworks tied to a cat's tail. time of ritual diminishment in a rural church, and the fuchsia going psycho where they scattered his ashes. time of *you can lead a horse across the border but you cannot...* time of screwing to fusion with the windows open in venice no less. time of a word coming loose with the give of elastic in an ankle sock. time of rinsing their spit from her hair in a school shower. time of saviours and hatemail and crying like a caravan on fire. time of the human league singing *leb-an-on! belfast*, by bony m. time of cher doing *gypsies, tramps and thieves*, and the boys at the bus stop doing *gypsies, tramps and thieves* until she riddles their leader's lip into blood. time of no time at all, long cycles of neglect and grind. time of flies on ruined fruit. time of skinning a knee in the stonebreakers' yard. time of lead lifters

waxing their aerial conjuries to angel. time of murals with
the eyes of mediaeval portraits, following you from one end
of an alley to another like a mad ancestor twice removed.
time of under the counter contraception, of bootleg records
in brown paper bags, *they don't play our songs on the radio,*
etc. time they staked a resurrection gate above the telluric
pulse of her tongue. time of bobbed apples and him standing
heliocentric in a system of charmed bees.

when else?

a seduction of humming wires leading her on to cities and
cities and cities. honey-buzzard, feathered desperado,
shrieking from a derelict watchtower. tart notes of quince
and burning charcoal. and kiss his intemperate headlong
under the juvenile willow like outlaws once. when love's
liquefaction fails her, and she sulks in stalemate's sackcloth
tearing hair. but also her gorgio husband's back in the bed
when she could spread his majesty like marmalade, loveliest
mensch. most of all, though, it is the nonsense of his coffin, a
puzzlebox unlocked only in the mineral tedium of sleep.

she went far from home.

with blunt eyes, yes. and says *you'd be amazed, when they're all laid out, just how many bones a body contains.*

so far from home?

but you know what they say? home is the lining of a coat. when you spread it out you're hanging your map on a branch. these territories will jut and suck and mushroom under any hand that tries to rub them out.

but can she live without her mountain?

yes. and no. tomorrow the gangrenous forest-future, making poets of us all. is hamlet's cod philosophy printed in a christmas cracker. is a million mouths begging the bare city bare. she'll be alright. she can't unlearn the black anchors of this arms, but sees how the tattoo parlour has emptied its anchors in favour of rainbows and butterflies, the gnomic allure of letters in a language no one here can speak. if she had the needle. if she could sew one foible phrase to her skin, it would be *hunger*, or *pivot*, or *sliabh*.

can the mountain live without her?

a name is what we measure the dead against, rolling them
out like bolts in a crowded bazaar and crying our wears to
the vaulted roofs of churches. there are only proddy church-
es here, immaculate and empty, the hollowed-out volcano
lairs of bond villains. what i mean is, a mountain is a kind of
scar. there are the scars of harm and then there are the scars
of loving too well. biddy's been singing his name through
this dizzy imperial city long time. she knows a rainbow
isn't painted or la-la-ed but walked. she's a survivor. see her
crooked teeth catch light, their irregular plates pushed into
a smile.

Love poem

for whom the horse is sacred. today the meadow,
reddish, vague with ice. woodsmoke, and i stare
over my shoulder into the declining sun; walk, open-
mouthed, into a cloud of thunder flies. i am trying
to be present; striding over the frozen ground.
ahead of me, a world of swift occlusions: night
things, stammeringly gratified. to feel even
the moon behind me, blue fist in the small of my
back, this burgeoning flint. to feel for a moment,
stunned, almost drowsy with fear. i know i have
wasted so much. somewhere there is wet sand
easing through an hourglass, an end to all my frugal
frenzies. peel a puckered skin from me; my opaque
mail of desperation. to wish i'd run with veterans
of a soft delving, had pushed my own tired
dark aside, a dexterous mole. *piano players'*

fingers, all their life refusing music. what a fool.
my brother asks how i can love the quality of light
behind the church? how i can love what i cannot
ever look directly at? oh, my dear, you are braver
than me. my love is this mute deflection. is just

aversion's avid thirst.

Animal affinities

The umbilical cord is regarded in the folklore of many
cultures as an anchor for the soul. It must never be thrown
away haphazardly. It should never be destroyed. What hap-
pens to the cord has a real, material bearing on the future
life of the child; it can bind them to a native place, it can
influence their destiny: bury the cord in a school yard for the
child to grow up a scholar, bury the cord in the grounds of a
church for the child to grow up devout. A cord may be kept
or worn, twisted into a charm for luck. It may be wrapped
and placed in water, if the child is to travel the world. When I
was born, my mother's shaggy black dog ate a portion of my
cord. I have belonged to the dog ever since.

By which I mean what? As a child I felt a deep affinity for
and a strong identification with the dogs in my life. My early

drawings were of dogs. My favourite stories had canine protagonists. In my games of make-believe I played at being a dog, or I incorporated the dogs around me, casting them as sidekicks, oracles and heroes. I was an avid collector of dog memorabilia, and an irritatingly precocious font of canid lore. My best companions were dogs; they were my lone constant, a reassuring presence in a life spent on the move.

Growing up, the local dogs ran fairly wild, where 'wild' is both a territory and a state of being. Escapes and impromptu matings were common, leading – the joy! – to litters of mongrel puppies. Out walking, you would often cross paths with a dog in the road. They were not strays, but they were not beholden to their owners either; those dogs enjoyed a freedom impossible today, and especially in London. I did not grow up in London; in many ways I too was wild, and *of* the wild. This wildness had both its sinister and idyllic aspects. I miss acutely, even now, the ability to roam the daylight into darkness. I miss the cliffs and beaches. I miss the commons and scrub forests. I miss the overgrown gardens of deserted houses where I'd pick ripe rhubarb and eat it raw. I miss the half-afraid thrill of the nighttime. I miss the haunted feeling of the quarries and the tors. Mine was not a cosseted or overly-scrutinised childhood. I miss the hours unaccounted for, those hours reserved for being and becoming lost.

There's more that I don't miss. The private lives of children are secretive and hazardous, and I felt I belonged to the wild in a way that the adults around me did not; this cut me off. The wild had its own rules, its own code of silence, it taught its own harsh lessons, especially to girls. The dogs in their sauntering freedom were vulnerable. We envied them, but they lived in proximity to danger; they represented danger too. We would follow a loose dog for hours, watching it lope its inscrutable errands. At times the dog would tire of us, turning to give chase, all hackles and teeth. We would scatter, then, whooping, delighted and scared. A dog was a riddle: simultaneously 'ours' and all its own. It had an independent existence, a peculiar self-possession.

I can't remember how old I was when I heard the word 'feral' for the first time, but I do remember that when I first heard it, it wasn't being applied to animals, but to people, specifically to children a lot like myself. I was twelve or thirteen when I read the hateful prohibition 'No Irish. No Blacks. No dogs' in a book. I was fifteen when I encountered its cousin in the real world: 'No dogs! No Gypos!' in the window of a shop. I saw it again at an all-night garage, and later in the doorway of a pub beneath a cutesy hanging horseshoe. I've seen in often since, and every time it strikes me that an equivalence is being drawn between certain kinds of people and certain kinds of animals. The idea of the dog is evoked in its most negative aspect, and the human 'other' is assumed to share those characteristics, to be dog-*like*: dirty and un-governable, teeming with fleas and unspecified menace.

Historically, representations of ethnic and cultural 'others' have tended to dehumanise their subjects. But depictions of Irish and Traveller people also conflate persons and their animals to an unusually high degree. In the iconography of anti-Irish racism, a dog of mean and cunning cast is both an extension of and a figure for the violence and cunning of the humans to which it belongs. The 'dangerous dog' in partic-ular provides a legitimating occasion for the expression of deeply held anxieties surrounding race and class: the mas-tiff or 'pit bull-type' dog does not merely posses a charac-teristic savagery; it is also material evidence of that quality in the people to whom the dog belongs. These people have bred that animal for fighting, they must surely mistreat it; they do not love the dog, they are merely using it as a 'status symbol', or to engender fear in others. These types of dis-course use both fear of the dog and 'concern' for its welfare as opportunities to express and confirm a variety of shared class and racial hatreds.

Because this realisation came to me in a faltering form during early adolescence, it made a dramatic and indelible impression, and once witnessed it was everywhere. Perhaps it *is* everywhere. In the world and in literature.

In a recent article Jeanne Dubino writes that dogs appear over fifty times in Bram Stoker's Dracula: they are his agents and emissaries; they advance his ambition to perpetuate his race and to create legions of semi-human followers. They're not characters, but they drive the plot, and entwine two central Victorian fears: the fear of rabies, and the fear of immigrants. In 1896, the year before Dracula was published, The Times reported that rabies in Ireland was 'rife'; it went on to speculate that dogs from Ireland were responsible for numerous outbreaks in England. In the collective conscious-ness of Victorian England the threat of rabies from Ireland was greater than from almost anywhere else in the world, and this notion was entirely related to the status of the Irish as uncivilised interlopers, barbarians at the gate. Dracula, himself an immigrant outsider, colonizes the colonizers through a supernatural virus that reduces his victims to a race of dog-like thrawls. His arrival in England is heralded by the appearance of a large black dog on the beach. Dubino suggests that Ireland and the contested Old World of Count Dracula are one and the same. This seems plausible to me.

I find myself wanting to go back further. In the *Topographia Hiberniae* by Gerald of Wales, written in or around 1188, the Irish are depicted as bestial beings who express their inhumanity through intercourse with animals. Werewolves are a significant feature of this text: a race of human-shaped Irishmen, with fur, teeth, and treachery beneath.

Further still, and it is not merely within anti-Irish propaganda that ideas of Irishness and caninity are linked. The Ulster Cycle's most famous mythic hero, Cú Chulainn, is himself simultaneously a man, a God, and an animal. Born Sétant, he becomes Cú Chulainn- 'hound of the forge' or 'Culann's hound' – when he kills Culann's beloved guard dog, and volunteers himself as a replacement. In battle Cú Chulainn prowls, pursues and fights with the ferocity of a dog, as if having taken on that animal's attributes. He is described as entering a rage-spasm, becoming warped, misshapen and monstrous, simultaneously more and less than human. Yet Cú Chulainn is also beautiful, desirable, a figure whose iconography both Republicans and Unionists have sought to claim for their own. He seems to shape-shift between the animal and the human; between God and mortal, as well as between political affinities.

Ambiguous God-dogs were a favourite theme of mine, and as a teenager I spent a great deal of time writing about and drawing them. This obsession was intensified after an early visit to the British Museum where I first saw stela of the jackal-headed Gods Anubis and Wepwawet. At the time, I don't think I had ever seen a real jackal, and had only a hazy idea of what they actually looked like. But the *idea* of the jackal was consuming, and, prone to magical thinking as I was, I felt an especial connection to them because my mother's name is Jacqueline.

In the First Dynasty Anubis was merely a protector of graves, but his legend gained power, and by the Middle Kingdom he was also an embalmer of the dead. He ushered souls into the afterlife and attended the scale in which the hearts of the dead were weighed. Those figures impress me still. They transmit that cool imperious otherness, which is the heart of all wild dogs. For the ancient Egyptians jackals were a common sight; they became associated with the dead because they were so often to be found scavenging in cemeteries. Unlike hyenas who became figures of abjection and taboo, the jackal was recuperated into myth, their connection to the bodies of the dead recast in a more solemn and benevolent guise. The jackal's ability to find the good part of old meat was the literal foundation for their role in the judgement of the deceased. Anubis' animal otherness was precisely what qualified him to weigh the hearts of mortal men, but his half-human aspect prevented awe from becoming revulsion and fear.

There are other dog-heads, cynocephali as they are properly called. In medieval Christianity saints with the heads of dogs were not uncommon. The idea of a cannibal and barbarous race of dog-like aspect, physically transfigured through baptism, is a potent allegory – and argument – for the redemptive power of faith, crusade and conversion. Saint Christopher in particular is portrayed with the head of a dog. Many scholars have pointed to depictions of the saint as a Christianised survival of the cult of Anubis: as saint Christopher protects travellers, so Anubis protects those embarked upon their final journey. It is a tenuous, but intriguing idea. It is generally supposed that the notion of Saint Christopher as a dog-headed giant resulted from a mistranslation of the Latin term 'Cananeus', meaning 'Cananite' as 'canineus', or 'canine'. I'm not sure why but the slipperiness of language and the protean nature of the saint's form seem to dovetail in a pleasing way to me. It just feels right. Perhaps it is something in my own unstable identity that responds so positively to this ambiguity. As children, my brother and I dealt with corresponding feelings of alienation in similar but opposite ways: my brother, who is high-functioning autistic, imagined himself as belonging to a superior alien race, whereas I felt a powerful kinship with the 'subhuman' or the animal. Neither of us felt recognised or accommodated within the remit of 'humanity', or by its several categories of ready-made belonging. We were beings without status, class, or territory. We were not liked or welcomed, and so we formed our own system of identification, with the marvellous and monstrous 'others' of literature and cinema.

For me it was werewolves, forever linked in popular imagination both to Ireland and to 'gypsies'; to the homeless, and to poor white trash. From the *Topographia Hiberniae* onwards werewolf narratives position the outlaw 'other' amongst us as both intrinsically magical and inherently violent. Werewolves are twice removed from 'normal' human society through the twin discourses of exoticism and degeneracy. Gerald of Wales coined the paradox: the Irish are naturally 'contra naturam'. Like Lady fucking Gaga, we were born this way. In popular horror, werewolves rarely got to be sexy or civilised. The vampire is white, wealthy, cultured and beautiful; vampires may be exiles but their estrangement from humanity is generally characterised by a kind of melancholy refinement. Werewolves on the other hand are predominantly figured as savage; their transformation is visceral and grotesque, something they are unable to control or to conceal. Werewolves reminded me of me; they are the white working-class women of fiction, unloved and unlovely, incapable of ever truly transcending the horror they become.

I felt looked at that way. It is what 'feral' meant: wear a white human skin all you want, but the truth will out, you're not one of us. My brother escaped the weight of that gaze by forging into the future at warp-speed. I sunk back into the Jacobean gloom of the 'Old World'. We talk about this often. He points out that the notion of lycanthropy as a medical condition resulting from depression was current as early as the seventh century. Trained as I was to see myself as abject and ugly, I felt a deep kinship with the abject and ugly of a fictional Gothic universe. A werewolf will often bear the curse of his ancestors. Or, more accurately, his ancestry constitutes that curse. I connect this to the long continuities of violence that form part of my cultural and familial heritage, and about which I have felt a persistent anxiety. I connect it also to the body as a site and source of shame: the grim contortions of my anorexia were a kind of lycanthropy for me, a morbid and deforming tussle inside my own skin for control.

All of which is complex, but might easily be reduced to one simple statement: I did not – do not – like people very much. I loved – and still love – the dogs in my life. I have always experienced most human interactions as demanding and bewildering at best. While people have a great capacity for love, they also have enormous potential for acts of arbitrary cruelty. They can manipulate and dissemble; they can – and usually will – torment and abuse those weaker than themselves for their own advancement or amusement. They instrumentalise and exploit the world, its creatures, and each other. They build fences and draw boundaries; they write laws to parade their bigotries as legal and moral right. It is, in all, fairly nauseating. Dogs offer a respite from that: they accept you as you are, they want very little from you, and they are naked in their motivations. Dogs have chosen to cooperate with us, to participate in our society, and they see good in us even when we can't.

I have friends who would describe themselves as 'cat people'. Which is fine. I don't hate cats. I don't hate any animal.

But I don't love them either. I remember reading about an archaeological dig in Greenland, where animal and human remains were found together, side by side, perished by famine. The graves showed evidence that dogs and their humans laid down and died together: the people would not eat the dogs, nor did the dogs consume their people in order to stave off hunger. Other corpses were found, where cats had gnawed their humans in an attempt to save themselves. This doesn't mean cats are bad, but I've often wondered about what's really being celebrated and enshrined when people laud or fetishize cats' 'independence' and – for want of a better word - selfishness. This has nothing to do with the animals themselves, only what we project onto them, the kinds of things we choose to value as a society. There aren't many cats in my poems, or when they appear, they are often allegorical capitalists, policemen, or judges. I feel a bit guilty about that, but I do still see my love of dogs as part and parcel of my socialism. I see dogs as my first socialist teachers. For dogs, cooperation is not merely a demonstration of kindness or affection, it is their mechanism of survival. I believe it is ours too, if only we knew it.

I was recently asked if I would remove 'dog-whisperer' from my updated author biography. I will not. My identity as a poet has not superseded or diminished this prior title. My

Hyena! Jackal! **Dog!**

relationship to my animals is an integral part of who I am as a writer, and of who I am as a person too. Saint Roch was attended by a dog when sick and homeless. In the temples of Asclepius in ancient Greece, sacred dogs would lick the wounds of petitioners hoping to be healed. I credit the dogs in my own life with similar feats of healing. I don't like to say that I 'train' dogs because the process is more reciprocal and complicated than that. On more than one occasion I feel that my dogs have 'saved' me.

Dogs, my own and others, feature heavily in my work, as subjects and as speakers. But more than this, I connect various modes or positions in writing to jackals and to dogs. The Jackal self in connected to the work of both judgement and grieving, her landscapes are often shaped by war and deprivation; she reckons with heritage, she mourns her dead. The Dog relates to the 'othering' of female outsiders, and to recuperation and recovery from the violence of that othering. Whatever else a Dog poem is about, it is also about love, for people and for places, and for something long despised within the self.

Acknowledgments

Thanks are due to Blue of Noon, Culture Matters, Magma, One Hand Clapping Magazine, Poetry Review, and Shearsman Magazine where some of these poems first appeared.

Lightning Source UK Ltd.
Milton Keynes UK
UKHW012154060122
396733UK00001B/52